R. hiely

Audio-Visual Media for
Education and Research
VOLUME 2

COMPUTERS FOR IMAGEMAKING

Audio-Visual Media for Education and Research Series

Already published

Volume 1: POLITICS AND THE MEDIA
Edited by M. J. Clark BA, PhD
University of Southampton

NOTICE TO READERS

'If your library has not already placed a standing/continuation order for this series, may we recommend that you place a standing/continuation order to receive all new volumes immediately on publication. Should you find that these volumes no longer serve your needs, you may cancel your order at any time without previous notice.

Related Journals of Interest

COMPUTERS AND GRAPHICS Editor: Larry J. Feeser
COMPUTERS AND EDUCATION Editors: David F. Rogers and P. R. Smith
LEONARDO Founder-Editor: Frank J. Malina

Specimen copies will gladly be sent upon request

Also of Interest

VISUAL ART, MATHEMATICS AND COMPUTERS - Selections from the
   Journal LEONARDO Edited by Frank J. Malina

COMPUTERS FOR IMAGEMAKING

Edited by

D. R. Clark, Ph.D.

University of London
Audio-Visual Centre

Published for the
British Universities Film Council Ltd

by
PERGAMON PRESS

OXFORD · NEW YORK · TORONTO · SYDNEY · PARIS · FRANKFURT

U.K.	Pergamon Press Ltd., Headington Hill Hall, Oxford OX3 0BW, England
U.S.A.	Pergamon Press Inc., Maxwell House, Fairview Park, Elmsford, New York 10523, U.S.A.
CANADA	Pergamon of Canada, Suite 104, 150 Consumers Road, Willowdale, Ontario M2J 1P9, Canada
AUSTRALIA	Pergamon Press (Aust.) Pty. Ltd., P.O. Box 544, Potts Point, N.S.W. 2011, Australia
FRANCE	Pergamon Press SARL, 24 rue des Ecoles, 75240 Paris, Cedex 05, France
FEDERAL REPUBLIC OF GERMANY	Pergamon Press GmbH, 6242 Kronberg-Taunus, Hammerweg 6, Federal Republic of Germany

First edition **1981**

British Library Cataloguing in Publication Data

Computers for imagemaking. - (Audio-visual media for education and research; vol.2).
1. Computer drawing
I. Clark, D R
II. British Universities Film Council
III. Series
001.6'443   T385   79-40426

ISBN 0-08-024058-5 **(Hardcover)**
ISBN 0-08-024059-3 **(Flexicover)**

In order to make this volume available as economically and as rapidly as possible the typescript has been reproduced in its original form. This method has its typographical limitations but it is hoped that they in no way distract the reader.

Printed and bound in Great Britain by
William Clowes (Beccles) Limited, Beccles and London

A NOTE ON THE SERIES

The interests of the British Universities Film Council extend far more widely than its name would suggest and embrace every aspect of the use and production of audio-visual media and materials at degree-level. For many years the Council has been committed to specialist publication and launched the series **Audio-Visual Media for Education and Research** to fill a gap in the literature.

The aim of the series is to provide hand-books in defined subject areas in which the production and use of audio-visual media are discussed by teachers, researchers and producers. The emphasis is on producing a varied and informative introduction to the subject, rather than attempting exclusive presentation of advanced research results.

The first volume in the series was **Politics and the Media : Film and Television for the Political Scientist and Historian.** This second volume, **Computers for Imagemaking,** was inspired by a BUFC conference of the same name which Dr David Clark co-ordinated. All the contributions have been specially commissioned for the book.

The views expressed are, of course, those of individual authors, not of the Council.

Plans are in hand for future volumes in the series and further information about the series and about the work of the Council may be obtained from The Director, British Universities Film Council Ltd, 81 Dean Street, London W1V 6AA, England.

NOTES ON CONTRIBUTORS

Dr David Rayner Clark is Senior Producer at the University of London Audio-Visual Centre and display consultant to the Interactive Planetary Image Processing Systems Group at University College, London.

Professor Richard Gregory heads the Brain and Perception Laboratory at the University of Bristol and has written widely on the subject of vision.

Dr Tom DeFanti is Professor of Information Engineering and Dan Sandin is from the School of Art and Design, both at the University of Illinois at Chicago Circle. They work together in the Electronic Visualization Laboratory.

Dr Edwin Catmull now works with Sprocket Systems Inc., a division of Lucasfilm. Previously he developed the Computer Graphics Laboratory at the New York Institute of Technology.

Dr Yehonathan Hazony is head of the Interactive Computer Graphics Laboratory in the School of Engineering at Princeton University.

Dr John C. Gilbert works in the Graphics Section of the University of London Computer Centre. He has collaborated with John Richmond on developing graphics for the Open University mathematics courses.

Dr John Richmond is Executive Producer, Mathematics, at the BBC-Open University Production Centre and has commissioned a large amount of computer graphics for the OU courses.

Dr Kenneth C. Knowlton, one of the pioneers of computer animation, has worked for some years at Bell Laboratories, New Jersey, and has produced many computer-generated films which are widely used in education and research.

FOREWORD

This book sets out to tell the computer **non-expert** all he or she needs to know in order to begin Computer Imagemaking. In the hands of expert computer engineers, computer picture drawing systems have, since the earliest days of computing, produced interesting and useful images. Recently there have been major developments in computer technology; the consequence of these developments is that now it no longer takes the skill of an expert computer engineer to draw pictures; anyone can do it, provided they know how to make use of the appropriate machinery.

The field of computer imagemaking is wide. Until comparatively recently, the final product was always cinema film, whether for use in advertising, education or for artistic productions. Recent developments have, however, expanded the field to include television as a useful output device, and the arrival of such systems as Teletext and Prestel means that computer-generated images will feature more and more prominently in our everyday lives. Medical diagnostic techniques, such as the Brain and Body scanners, use analogue image display for the digitally computed images of sections through the body, and images of the earth taken from cameras on artificial satellites are becoming more accessible, especially for weather forecasting.

This book reflects the diversity of the field. The specially-commissioned articles cover not only the technological and cost factors but also some problems in the perception of images and their use in teaching and research.

The aim of the book is to provide the context for, and fundamental information on, the generation of images by computer. After reading it, the student, artist or film-maker should be ready to ask the right questions, express the project in appropriate terms and know where to go for facilities and advice.

ACKNOWLEDGEMENTS

This book arose from the 1978 Annual Conference of the British Universities Film Council. The then Director, Yvonne Renouf, asked me to organise a strand of that conference to introduce non-specialists to the field of computer imagemaking. My introduction to the field came whilst teaching chemistry at The University of Toronto. Students in Professor J.C. Polanyi's group made a film in 1968 to show the dynamics of chemical reactions. Each frame was plotted on paper and photographed; it was a labour of love and there had to be a better way. At the University of London Audio-Visual Centre, the Director, Michael Clarke, has encouraged me to explore the field and I am grateful to him for that opportunity. My collaboration with Dr J.F.Wilson on the use of stereoscopic imaging for computed molecular structures has provided a practical opportunity for programming, and membership of the Interactive Planetary Image Processing System (IPIPS) team under Dr Garry Hunt at University College, London, has given me the chance to examine at first hand the latest developments in Image Processing.

The present Director of the British Universities Film Council, Elizabeth Oliver, oversaw the Conference and suggested that from it should come the second volume in the series **Audio-Visual Media for Education and Research**. As its Editor, I have the responsibility for the content, but the form of the book and its careful presentation are her work. I am very grateful to her for the time and attention she has given to its preparation for publication.

Nina McNeill composed the pages and accepted my many last-minute emendations with patience and understanding. I should also like to thank Paul Wilkes and Penny Hollow for their advice and expertise in the preparation of my diagrams for printing and also Penny Henry who typed my contributions.

Finally, I am indebted to the other contributors to this volume. Without their work, the field of computer imagemaking would be far less interesting than it is.

David R. Clark
May 1980

CONTENTS

This picture, and the picture on page 28, are images of the earth from space. They were obtained from the METEOSAT satellite on **5 November 1978** at Noon GMT. This satellite is geostationary above 0° Lat, 0° Long. and sends three such pictures every thirty minutes. This is the image in the visible region of the spectrum. The earth being a globe, England, at between 55 and 60° North of the equator, is almost invisible, as well as being covered with clouds. Nevertheless images such as these are enormously useful for weather forecasting and climatology. At the Laboratory for Planetary Atmospheres, University College, London, Dr R. Saunders in Dr Garry Hunt's team is examining the most useful ways of treating such data using the IPIPS facility. Sequences of these images can be combined, after some processing to equalise the contrast ranges, to show the time-course of cloud development. A movie-loop of these images reveals both the global and local features of the weather in a most dramatic way.

Pictures of this kind are already the result of image processing. The signals representing the brightness of a point across the scanline of the imagemaking device in the satellite have been encoded, transmitted to a receiving station in Germany, re-assembled into an image and processed to remove any unwanted distortions incorporated by the camera system.

THE TECHNICAL FOUNDATIONS OF
COMPUTER IMAGEMAKING

David R. Clark
University of London Audio-Visual Centre

The recent history of computer imagemaking is, to a large extent, the history of the development of new technologies. The constraints which these technologies impose have determined both the style and process of computer imagemaking. A clear understanding of these factors, and an appreciation of the mechanisms of perception, are prerequisites for the study of picture making by computer. This chapter seeks to provide an introduction to the field.

The rate of appearance of new ideas in the various fields in which computers are used for imagemaking may just be beginning to decrease. The subject is beginning to stabilize. The preceding 20 years have witnessed an explosive growth in both the range and number of devices on which images can be created by computation. Whole classes of problems, like the hidden surface problem, were first posed, then solved, during this period, and there is now a recognised academic discipline called 'Computer Graphics', for want of a better title. As is always the case with a 'new' field of enquiry, it is the coming together of people with different backgrounds but a common interest that generates an explosion of creativity. No one person can claim the credit for starting the subject up; when the time is ripe, the process of nucleation seems to happen in several places almost simultaneously. There is no doubt, however, that the group formed by Ivan Sutherland at the University of Utah in the late 1960's has had a profound effect on the outlook of the field as we find it today. This is true of both the developments in machines for displaying images and for the strategies by which images may be most efficiently computed and ordered for plotting.

The decrease in the rate of decrease of computer memory cost, combined with the approach to the limit of switching speed of semiconductor junctions, makes it easier to predict the form that image display devices will take over the next twenty years. We are nearing the end of the innovation phase of computer imagemaking and are entering the period in which a large number of new applications for these imaging capabilities will be found and exploited.

THE VARIETY OF COMPUTED IMAGES

At this moment, computer generated images are already being used for a wide range of applications. For example, an expensive, but cost-effective, use is to simulate the views from the cockpit of an aircraft as the pilot 'flies' the aeroplane; it is cheaper to crash a simulator than a 747.

The movie industry in Hollywood has seen the potential for films produced entirely by machine, and no Sci-Fi feature is complete without its computer-animation-type pictures. The verisimilitude that is now attainable in computed images, if time and money are readily available, justifies the faith of the financial backers of the cinema; Edwin Catmull, in Ch. 4 sets out some of the problems in this area that are still to be overcome.

Simulation and movie-making are both attempts to generate images of 'real world' objects entirely mathematically. The camera has been replaced by a mathematical model. There is another field of computer imaging where the data is from some kind of camera, but the pictures have to be processed to be used. Two examples of this are the images from computer tomography — the 'brain scanner' and 'body scanner' images — and the pictures of Earth and Jupiter telemetered back from cameras aboard space craft.

These applications of computer imaging are often referred to as **Image processing**. The techniques that are used to display such images are no different from those used in simulators or movie-making; the main difference is that rather than being created to convey information, these images are examined and processed to extract the information that they contain. Here the major theoretical problems are in the fields of pattern recognition and artificial intelligence and novel picture-processing computers have been developed to speed the computations required.

A consideration of the problems of image analysis exposes one of the growth points for the next decade. The physiology of perception is just beginning to reveal the way that we construct mental images from the information impinging on the retina. An understanding of the way in which we see may suggest new and more efficient strategies for computing and presenting images.

Images, or pictures, can be thought of as at least 4-dimensional quantities. In addition to the two spatial dimensions of the image plane, an image has a temporal dimension. A 'still' picture is just a special case of this temporal sequence in which there is no change in the image from one instant to the next. A fourth dimension is the brightness, or intensity, of any point in the image at some instant. This brightness may be intrinsic to the object, or be a consequence of projecting a 3-space structure into the two dimensions of the image plane, or both. Extra dimensions are required to specify any colour that the image may have. A measure of the complexity of an image is the extent to which these dimensions can be portrayed. For example, adequate simulations of an emergency landing on an airfield known to the pilot require images that range over all the degrees of freedom. They must be large, change with time, and be good representations of the scene, both in terms of detail and colour. At the other end of the scale of complexity are the static, single intensity monochrome images to be seen on a Visual Display Unit, or, slightly more complex, the 'video games', whose images change (slightly) with time.

Between these two extremes lie the rest of the computer generated images. Images in which the degrees of freedom are considerably restricted tend to be called 'computer graphics'. These include the 'teletext' and 'viewdata' images, business graphics, the images of computer-assisted learning and the simpler examples of computer-aided design. There are no hard and fast divisions, but the limiting factors that delineate each group are almost always the limits imposed by the available technology.

There has never been a time when computers have not been used to produce images of some sort. Crude typographical images using a teleprinter, or dire renditions of the Mona Lisa from a line printer have always adorned computer room walls. They are on the one hand a tribute to the ingenuity of programmers and on the other a savage indictment of their artistic sensibilities. Nevertheless, the existence of such pictures is significant: there is an overwhelming urge to create images as a result of intellectual activity.

MODES OF DRAWING

There are two distinct modes that can be adopted for drawing images. These are now called the **Vector** and **Raster** systems. There have been several strands woven into the development of each mode. All the earliest systems, the teletype and the line-printer, were raster systems. This was because the writing head could only write in one direction across the paper and the paper could only be transported one way, up, past the head. The latest generation of machines are raster based, and this is to be the dominant technology for the rest of the century, but in that middle period of explosive development the only worthwhile device was the calligraphic, or vector plotter.

VECTOR SYSTEMS

The difference between the systems is not primarily one of technology. There is an important philosophical difference. A rasterised image has the property that the strategies used to encode, transmit and display it are in principle independent of the content of the image itself. On the other hand, a vectorised image is composed of only that information which is required to form the image. For example, it takes just as much time to transmit a television image of a completely blank screen as it does to transmit an image full to capacity with picture detail. The scanning raster must be completed in the same way in each case. The entire image is encoded in a form that bears no relation to what the image contains.

On the other hand, the instructions required to draw nothing on a vector device contain at the most a few orders to move on to the next image. At the other extreme of vector plotting, the more detailed the image, the more instructions there have to be in the plotting file.

These fundamental differences relate directly to the computational nature of the images. The logic of computing the image of a mathematical object is that the computation computes **something**. Some point or region of the object is transformed into some point or region in the image. A very large class of objects can be represented as a framework of straight lines. This fact is very useful because the projection of a straight line from the object into the plane of its image is also a straight line. Thus the computation of these objects can just become the computation of a number of lines. Since, until very recently, all computation has been by the serial processing of stored instructions, the output of an image computation is a string of information about the intersections of these lines. All the regions of the image plane that are not contributed to in this way by the image of the object are unspecified. This stream of data is ideally suited to vector drawing devices since they only draw lines. A raster device, on the other hand, must be instructed to draw 'nothing' on the raster path just as it must be instructed to draw 'something'.

The name **vector** for these plotting devices derives from the fact that a straight line is defined by its end-points. Since the end of one line is usually the start of the next, the commands to the plotter are always at least a pair of numbers representing the x and y values of the next endpoint. Mathematically, this pair is referred to as a vector, since it specifies a line of a given length in a given direction.

The list of all the vectors to be plotted is held in the plot file, and the organisation of this file so as to allow the updating of the picture with the minimum of effort is a very important part of the design of vector plotting systems.

Mechanical Plotters

The earliest vector-drawing machines were x-y paper plotters. Since they were designed to produce an ink-on-paper image, the time taken by the pen to reach a particular point from any point on the table was chosen with more regard to the positional accuracy to be achieved than to the total time required to draw an image. For still images, precision is more important than speed of drawing. We shall see later that this is not the case for images forming a sequence to convey the impression of motion.

As the need to draw larger numbers of images grew, mainly from the pressure from computer users wanting to make movie sequences, an alternative to photographing the paper plots one frame at a time had to be found. Looking back, it is remarkable that some of the pioneer computer film makers had the patience to photograph literally thousands of images one after the other.

The major factor controlling the speed of paper plotting was, and is, the mechanical movement of the pen. The pen was moved to its new position by motors controlled from analogue or, later, digital signals derived from the difference between the current [x,y] co-ordinates of the pen and the computer co-ordinates of the next point to be drawn. Since these calligraphic devices were designed to draw straight lines from the current to the next position, any attempt to portray a curve was limited by the extent to which the curve could satisfactorily be approximated by a number of short chords. The incremental nature of this style of plotting imposed a high level of mechanical precision on the device if the path traced out by a large number of line segments representing a circle, for example, was to close on itself accurately.

Light-emitting Plotters

An electron beam has effectively no inertia and so can be repositioned very fast. Used to excite a phosphor, as in an oscilloscope or TV tube, the path swept out by the electron beam could be made to leave a trail of light. There are three ways of making this trail 'permanent'.

Firstly, it can be used to expose photographic emulsion. This is the basis of the **Microfilm Recorder**. The film acts as the integrator to remove the decay-time of the phosphor. The point of light, tracing out the computed line segments for either seconds or hours, generates a final image in the film emulsion. This can be printed onto paper or projected onto a screen.

Secondly, the image can be frozen for a reasonable length of time onto the face of a special **storage tube**. This system has a large number of disadvantages that are set out in the chapter by DeFanti and Sandin but, because it was the only device available at the crucial time, it has formed the basis of a large number of systems and even today still has its adherents. This device was for display technology what FORTRAN was to the programmer — terrible for the job but (just) better than nothing. Only now are a generation of users coming up who are not blinkered by contact with either the storage tube or FORTRAN.

The third system of making this trail of light 'permanent' is to repeat the drawing of the image sufficiently fast to utilise the persistence of vision of the eye. This is the **Refreshed Display**. The physiology and psychology of the persistence of human vision is very complicated. The impression of 'flicker' depends on the size of the flickering image on the retina, whether it is in central or peripheral vision, whether it is coloured or monochrome, and on the relative contrasts both within the flickering image and between the image and its surroundings.

The most familiar devices that rely on the persistence of vision for their effect are the cinema and television. It is common knowledge that cinema film is projected at 24 frames per second. What is not so widely known is that this is not the rate at which the pictures are flashed on the screen. It is usual to flash every frame on and off three times; there is a three-bladed shutter spinning round in the light path once every 1/24th second, so the flicker rate is 72 images/second. The choice of 24 frames per second has more to do with the de-blurring of motion and the sensitivity of early film emulsions than with the persistence of vision effect under the viewing conditions found in a cinema.

These considerations have not been carefully applied to the repetitive drawing of the computed vector display image. A very fast vector drawing system might draw 5000 short vectors/second. Assuming a picture rate of 25/second, this might suggest that a picture composed of 200 vectors could be drawn sufficiently rapidly so as to appear not to flicker. There are two points here. Firstly, not a great deal can be drawn with 200 vectors. It might represent 20 circles each with 10 segments, a goodish approximation for circles whose diameter is less than 1/10 of the picture width. Secondly, at this rate, each point is refreshed every 1/25 second; moreover, its nearest neighbour is only refreshed at the same rate, so, unless the display subtends a small angle at the viewer's eye and is not highly contrasted with its surroundings, it may flicker objectionably. Real-time vector drawing is, then, rather restricted.

Brightness Variation in Vector Displays

The early electronic vector plotting devices were just simulations of the paper x-y plotters. They therefore carried over into the phosphorescent image system an unnecessary restriction. All parts of a line had to have the same intrinsic brightness. There are two ways to circumvent this limitation. The crudest is to draw over, or just beside, the previous line to make it brighter; the other method is to modulate the beam current during its passage along the vector. This last technique has practical limitations as well as requiring an alteration in the form of the data structure of the image. The deflection fields required to move the beam to its new position depend on the charge in the beam and rather complicated compensation circuitry is required to maintain high positional precision.

There is a practical variant of this second method. It is to vary the deflection rate. So long as the persistence of vision criteria are satisfied, slowing the traverse along the vector has the visual effect of brightening the line. However, this technique wastes valuable plotting time and serves only to reduce the total number of vectors that can be refreshed. These 'dwell time' techniques cannot work for storage tube displays. If the recording device is photographic film, rather than the eye, and there is no need to expose the film in less than 1/24 second, the technique of spending longer over lines that have to be brighter is a good one. In most modern microfilm plotters, where the vectors are constructed by brightening up dots on a very fine grid of points to form the line, the exposure is controlled by the number of times each individual point is flashed. An excellent survey of the various vector techniques that have been developed is to be found in Newman & Sproull, 2nd Edition 1979.

RASTER SYSTEMS

There are two strands woven into the development of raster display systems. The first is the desire to make use of the television system as a display device for computers. The second is that certain important calculations about an image, for example the determination of the visibility of surfaces in the 2-D projection of a 3-D object, are easier if the image plane can be treated as a raster. This discovery of the scan-line algorithms has swung the balance away from vector displays as the natural mode of display.

Video Rasters

Television is an example of a raster refresh display. In this case the persistence of vision has been taken carefully into account in the design of the display. Television images are presented at a similar picture rate to films. Their image rates are also similar but the way this is achieved is quite different. The picture rate for NTSC-standard television, found in those parts of the world over which England and Germany have no financial or political control, is 30 complete pictures per second. The rest of the civilised world receives 25 complete TV pictures per second. In both cases the complete frame is transmitted as two interlaced fields, so that the image rates are respectively 60 and 50 images per second. Since the pictures are transmitted a line at a time, starting at the top of the picture and working down, adjacent lines in the frame are drawn 1/50 second apart, although the time betweeen drawing every second line is 1/25 second. Since the scanning of the image on the face of the camera tube is done twice to cover the whole area, the interlaced field will be different from the first scan if any motion has taken place within the time it takes to scan one field. Thus, in general, unlike the 3 identical flashes of the cinema frame, the two 'flashes' of the TV fields may be slightly different. This helps to smooth motion but may give rise to inter-field flicker at 50Hz. This is easy to perceive at high contrast ratios in low ambient illumination and can be very trying to the eye.

The number of lines in the video raster varies from system to system. There are again two dominant standards:

| NTSC | 60 fields/sec; | 262½ lines/field; | 2 fields/frame. |
| PAL | 50 fields/sec; | 312½ lines/field; | 2 fields/frame. |

Both of these systems have an aspect ratio for the picture area of 4 x 3. The only useful correspondence between these two systems is that their respective line frequencies are almost identical. This fact has made the conversion of images in one type of system to the other possible, though very difficult.

The Frame Buffer

The price paid to secure the independence from picture content of the encoding system is very high. The data rate required to sustain a video raster is very large in comparison with the data rates within conventional computers. This is easy to see by considering the resolution obtainable from a PAL raster. The resolvable points must be represented by at least 1 digital bit of data.

The PAL raster contains 625 lines in a complete field but not all of these contain picture information. Some 22 lines at the start of each field and about 3 at the end are within the **field blanking** period of 25 lines. Thus in the complete raster only 575 lines are used to contain picture information. Since the aspect ratio of this picture area is 4 x 3, each line must be composed of 768 points if horizontal and vertical definition are to be the same. This gives the total number of resolvable points, as, in in theory, 441600.

Digital data representing the intensity values of each of these points must be supplied every 1/25 second. However, this data must be supplied at the right moment in the raster and the true data rate is calculated by noting that 768 pieces of information must arrive during the drawing of one line. To allow for the electron beam to be re-positioned at the start of the next line after completing the previous scan, a **line blanking** period of $12\mu s$ is allowed in the total line period of $64\mu s$. Thus the data rate of a PAL TV line that has identical horizontal and vertical resolution is 768 points in $52\mu s$, i.e. 14.77 million point values/sec. This is 1.85 Mby/sec if each point can be either 'on' or 'off' and these bits are packed into 8-bit bytes. Although just possible on very powerful computers, such data rates impose a great strain, all for a very poor picture.

The corresponding figures for the NTSC system are a 'raster' of 480 x 640 = 307200 points and a 1-bit point rate of 1.54 Mby/sec.

The only way to bridge the gap between the rates of computation and display is to construct a **frame buffer**. This is easiest to imagine as a piece of fixed store (originally a spinning disc) that is continually being read as a raster at video rates whilst independently being written to at a much slower pace and in the order most suited to the computation in hand. Thus, as the buffer gradually fills with the picture information, the picture displayed at video rates appears to develop in the sequence in which the picture elements, or **pixels** are loaded.

Film Rasters

As in the case of the vector plotters, if the rquirement of speed can be relaxed, film serves as an ideal 'frame buffer'. Very high-definition rasters can be drawn using a vector plotter and this is the best method to date of generating high quality images.

Line Drawing on Raster Displays

If the individual pixels in the raster are resolved, as they must be if the full resolution of the display is to be obtained, a very serious defect in the raster display appears. A diagonal line, 1 pixel wide, appears to have jagged edges. This phenomenon is referred to as **aliasing**. This is a term taken from the theory of sampling. The digital representation of a smooth line by the nearest available grid-square automatically introduces an error of position.

Mathematically, this representation of the line is the result of (two-dimensional) sampling at a (spatial) frequency, f_s, set by the pixel separation. The sampling theorem shows that, with perfect sampling and perfect reconstruction, the highest frequency that can accurately be recovered is $f_s/2$. Frequencies higher than this appear at and below the sampling frequency (i.e. under an alias) and distort the reconstruction. The smooth line appears as one with jagged edges.

Several strategies exist for minimising the visual impact of these 'jaggies' that are referred to in the literature as **Anti-aliasing**. The underlying objective in all these strategies is to remove from the digital signal any transitions that involve higher spatial frequencies than the display raster can, in theory, resolve. If two adjacent pixels have values representing the extremes of the intensity range, e.g. 'o' in one and '255' in the next, an 'ideal' display should produce a hard line between the two pixels exactly at the pixel boundary. The difficulties arise when the 'hard line' should, from the point of view of the image, occur not at the pixel boundary, but at some intermediate point across the pixel. Since the resolution of the display is 'to the nearest pixel', these intermediate points imply a higher spatial frequency than is available. When they are implied in this way, they must be averaged out.

An infinitely fast transition is represented, in a Fourier Series summation, by contributions from an infinite number of the harmonics of the sampling frequency. Truncating the number of harmonics that are taken into account is what gives rise to the distortion, or aliasing. Sampling theory shows that if, instead of just truncating the harmonic series at some point, the whole spectrum is weighed by a particular function, $\sin(x)/x$, the resulting average, when displayed as a pixel raster, contains none of the high frequencies that give rise to aliasing. (The appropriate 2-D form of this function is shown in Fig. 2 of Chapter 6).

This technique, called **Spatial Filtering**, has proved very valuable in increasing the visual acceptibility of images. Objectively, the images are slightly blurred everywhere, as all the hard transitions have been smoothed out; subjectively, the image seems more acceptable. This subjective response reflects the fact that human vision appears to have built in to it the **reverse** of this filtering process: the eye 'sharpens up' blurred transitions. It is this property of the human visual system that makes the original aliased pictures so objectionable.

Sampling theory has considerable relevance to computer imagemaking and some familiarity with the subject is always valuable.

THE CONTROL OF BRIGHTNESS

There is a central problem in generating and recording images of variable brightness. That is the non-linear response of the eye or photographic emulsions to light. Nearly all electronic display technology is based as far as possible on linear devices, since, within the machine, signals have to be amplified and inter-related and this is most simply accomplished if all stages are linear.

For a large portion of the range of sensitivity of both the eye and the film emulsions, the relationship between stimulus and response is logarithmic. To double the density in a film, it is not nearly sufficient to double the exposure; similarly, doubling the amount of light reaching the eye does not result in the perception that the brightness of the light has doubled.

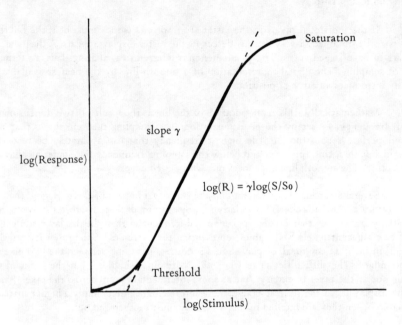

The index of sensitivity of response to stimulus is the exponent γ, the 'gamma' of the light-sensitive system.

A great deal of confusion centres around the various usages of 'gamma'. Here is a reproduction of a transparency generated on a microfilm plotter in which care was taken to generate regular steps of density. (Density in film is equivalent to log (output) in video since density is the integral of fractional absorption through the film):

A microdensitometer trace shows that the steps are indeed equal, but we do not report a uniform **visual** sensation; for example, the mid-point of the brightness does not **appear** to be in the centre of the density wedge.

The linear steps in density, acting as the stimulus for the eye, do not produce a linear response. The steps in exposure necessary to produce a uniform apparent gradation, rather than a uniform change in density, requires a second logarithmic transformation, with a different γ and S_o.

This problem, created by having several consecutive stages, each with its own γ and S_o, becomes acute in the television chain. Here, each camera tube in a 3-colour TV system will have a different γ, the television display tube has a similarly fixed but different γ and the whole system must be adjustable to produce an overall γ that gives a visually acceptable rendering of the brightness and colour of the original scene.

To a reasonable degree of approximation, provided that the values of γ for each stage in the chain lie in the range $2.5 > \gamma > 0.5$, the chain, taken as a whole, responds as if it had an effective gamma formed by the **product** of all the elementary gamma values.

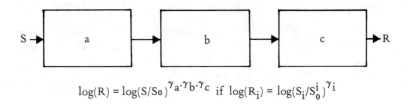

$$\log(R) = \log(S/S_o)^{\gamma_a \cdot \gamma_b \cdot \gamma_c} \text{ if } \log(R_i) = \log(S_i/S_0^i)^{\gamma_i}$$

Until recently, gamma correction has not been considered by computer imagemakers. The time has come to incorporate it. Treating the various stages, from the computation of an image to its presentation to the eye, as a system, this system should have an overall gamma of unity. It is wise to treat the final image display stage as having a specified, fixed, gamma. For example, the standard domestic TV tube has $\gamma_D \sim 2.2$. This requires, then, that in a TV chain, the product of the remaining component gamma values must be ~ 0.455.

In the normal TV chain, cameras have gamma values of $\gamma_T \sim 0.65$. To meet the requirement $\gamma_T \gamma_D \gamma_C \sim 1$, the value of γ_C, the gamma correction, must be ~ 0.7. Since this correction is applied at the camera head, from the point of view of the rest of the system, cameras, and hence other video input, must have $\gamma \sim 0.455$.

The consequences that follow from a failure to match the γ of computed images to the display device are most serious for continuous tone reproduction and colour fidelity. The digital data may contain $2^8 = 256$ discrete brightness levels. Even if the display device can, in principle differentiate satifactorily between these levels, it may not do so if these 256 equally spaced intervals are not transformed into a suitable set for display. The $\gamma_D \sim 2$ for the display means that at high brightness levels, the difference in brightness for equal steps in incoming electrical signal is very much larger than the change in brightness produced by the same sized step at low brightness levels. The scale becomes 'squeezed down' at the low brightness end. The transformation required, then, of the digital data is that it be 'presqueezed so that, after expanding by the display, the steps are again uniform. The appropriate transformation has, in this case, the gamma value ~ 0.46 and it is customary to normalize the two scales at 'white'.

A major source of confusion in this area is that, although a television picture tubehas a 'best' value of γ_D, this can be varied somewhat by the two controls **Brightness** and **Contrast**. To a first approximation, Brightness varies S_o, the threshold, and Contrast varies γ. (I have been taught that Brightness = Blackness and Contrast = Whiteness; it is a good rule for setting up monitors!). The stability and reliability of picture monitors is now such that once set up correctly on a calibrated test signal, they can be left alone. If there **seems** to be a need to twiddle these knobs to get a good picture, look somewhere else for the fault or error!

To summarize the current state of affairs, then, there are still two basic types of output device:

Mode	Devices	Features
1. Vector drawing	x-y paper plotters microfilm recorders	good for line drawing bad for area filling
2. Raster drawing	VDUs (Line printers) microfilm recorders	reasonable for line drawing good for area filling

The complicating factor is that a vector-drawing device can always draw a raster.

Mode	Real-time	Stored-time
Vector	Picture system II	FR80, CalComp 1670 D48
Raster	video framebuffer	D48 large frame buffers

The microfilm plotters like the FR80 and the Dicomed D48 have a resolution that permits the writing of 4000-line rasters. There are sometimes advantages in working in the image space as though it were a raster. The problems of hidden surface elimination and, to a certain extent, texturing, have efficient algorithms for their solution in this space. These factors, together with the opposing pressures to achieve simultaneously high definition and high speed of plotting, have focussed attention in recent years on raster based display systems.

COLOUR DISPLAYS

With the exception of the ink plotters, in which pens or ink jets marking in different colours can be used, all the devices so far described have been 'monochrome'. The generation of coloured images is possible in both vector and raster devices but it is by no means straightforward.

Colour Images from Microfilm Plotters

The technology of colour film is not straightforward. There are, broadly speaking two types of film:

a. Reversal Stock	— exposure and processing of this stock produces an image which, when viewed in transmission, reproduces the colour of the original scene (as best it can).
b. Negative Stock and print Stock	— these films, designed to be used as matched pairs, result in a print which, when viewed in transmission, reproduce the colours of the original scene.

The basic philosophy of print stock, or processed reversal stock, is that colour rendering is achieved by **subtraction** of colour from the light of the projector lamp. Thus the principal colour components for film dyes are the **Subtraction primaries:**

'- red'	=	'blue'	+	'green'	=	'cyan'
'- blue'	=	'green'	+	'red'	=	'yellow' (orange)
'- green'	=	'red'	+	'blue'	=	'magenta'

For each piece of colour-sensitive film there are two distinct parameters.

1. The spectral sensitivity of the emulsion layer
2. The spectral transmission of the resulting dye.

These are rarely the same, and the art, for such it is, of making a colour film stock is the adjustment of the relative sensitivites of each colour-sensitive component to wavelength in order to match the resulting variation of the absorption coefficient with wavelength in such a way as to produce a composite emulsion that gives the required overall characteristic.

There is a further complicating factor. Commercial films are designed for use with the light sources most commonly encountered − Sunlight and Tungsten light. The distribution of energy across the range of visible frequencies is very different for these two sources. This variation in energy, often measured by the quantity **Colour Temperature**, together with the non-uniform sensitivity of the emulsion to wavelength, means that individual emulsions must be tailored to suit each kind of light.

The task of creating a coloured image on film using a microfilm plotter becomes, then, one of computing the three images, one for Red, one for Green and one for Blue, and presenting them in succession to the film such that the intensity and wavelength distributions for each colour exactly matches that for which the emulsion being exposed has been designed. There are three distinct phases to this task:

1. Decomposing the image into the appropriate fraction of each primary.

2. Displaying each of these fractions on the phosphor tube in correct registration at the appropriate brightness and

3. Filtering the light from the phosphor to give the expected wavelength distribution for the emulsion.

Note that stages 2 and 3 are inter-related. Suppose, as an extreme case, that the light emitted from the tube phosphor contained no wavelength in the 'red' region of the spectrum. This is not impossible, since this represents a high-energy 'blue-green' phosphor often employed to give sufficient energy to expose very fine-grained (high resolution) black & white emulsions that are inherently insensitive. In this case, there is no appropriate brightness for the red fraction as there is no 'red' light from the phosphor. Less extreme cases require the matching of the brightness of the component image with the spectral distribution of the writing phosphorescence, taking into account the effect of the filter.

Stage 1, the decomposition of the computed image into the 3 primaries, relies on the theory of colour for its success. An excellent treatment of the theory of colour is given in **The Reproduction of Colour** by R. Hunt. The central feature of this theory is that it is usually possible to decompose a colour into 3 separate components such that, by recombining these components, the original colour is recovered.

It is by no means clear why this decomposition works. Any 'colour' has three defining properties, usually called **Hue**, **Saturation** and **Brightness**. There is a growing body of evidence based on the fact that the human eye has both colour-sensitive and 'monochrome' receptors (the **cones** and **rods** respectively in the retina), to suggest that the decomposition of incoming light into 3 separate colour components is not essential to the **interpretation** of a retinal image.

The relationship between the triples [Red, Green, Blue] and [Hue, Saturation, Brightness] is quite subtle and worth understanding.

Since display technology is at present geared to presenting red, green and blue images simultaneously to provide a sensation of colour, these will be read as the basic reference frame. Since only the three primary colours are required (a primary colour is one that cannot be composed from the other two chosen primaries; this allows a wide range of choice), the value of any colour, C, can be expressed as the algebraic sum of three components, say:

$$C = R + G + B$$

where the primaries are taken to be a Red, a Green and a Blue. This is equivalent to:

$$1 = R/C + G/C + B/C = r + g + b$$

where r, g and b are the **fractions** of each component in the colour. Using this notation, all colours lie in the triangular plane in the colour cube.

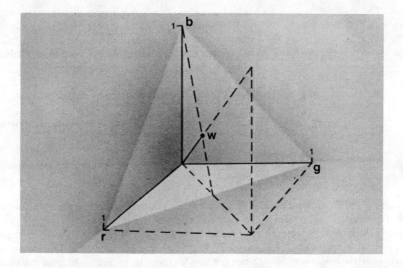

In this colour surface there is one point representing white. In this case w represents equal fractions of R, G and B. This 'white' contains no 'brightness' information. It refers to any grey between black and white that has the given **fractions** of R, G and B. This suggests that for black and white at least, brightness information can be separated from colour information.

The eye, although very good at discerning colour, is not perfect. Not all the points in the triangular surface are accessible. The gamut of human colour vision is well represented by the CIE (Commission Internationale D'Eclairage, 1933) diagram. As normally presented, this is shown as the projection of the sloping plane onto the (horizontal) [r, g] surface. A reasonable colour reproduction of this, courtesy of the General Electric (Lamp business division) Co. can be found in **Digital Image Processing**, Addison Wesley 1977.

To return to the problem of the separation of brightness from the other components of a colour C. The variation of brightness can be represented as points on one line in colour space:

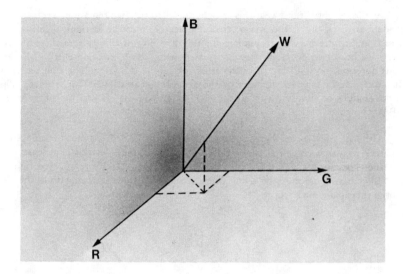

The axes of the graph are not the fractions, but the **absolute values** of R, G and B. The line W is composed of all those 'colours' with the same **fractions** of R, G and B, and so represents the whole range of 'brightness', at least for 'white'.

If there are to be two more quantities characterising the colour, apart from its brightness, they should be independent of this brightness. Since the triple [R, G, B] is sufficient to characterise any colour, then (if the system is linear, so beware 'gamma') other triples which are linear combinations of these primaries will also describe the colour. As 'brightness' appears to be one such combination, what are the others?

To guarantee their independence from brightness, they **must** lie in the plane **normal** to the direction of brightness. (Red and Green in the diagram lie in the plane normal to Blue, since they are independent of it). To be a worthwhile part of the system, this plane must pass through the origin of co-ordinates (Black; nothing of anything).

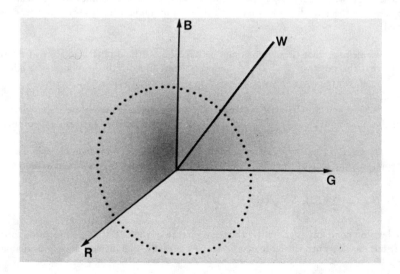

Just as the brightness vector is at right angles to the two remaining vectors, so, if they are to be independent of each other, these two remaining vectors must be at right angles in this plane. In principle, there is an infinite number of choices for the direction of this pair; is there a natural choice? To date, there have been two different answers (not counting the pioneering work of Schrödinger and Munsell) to this question, both arising from the study of colour television. The first based on the slight differences in visual acuity between colours of the same brightness (the NTSC choice). The second is based on the possibilities of simplification of decoder design and the elimination of error in hue reproduction (the PAL choice).

Although they are mathematically equivalent, the PAL solution is quite interesting. In the diagram, the G axis has been extended backwards. This extends, mathematically at least, the plane containing only B and G backwards, and there must be some line where the plane of zero brightness and this plane intersect. Similarly, there must be a line where a similar plane containing no B, the [R, G] plane, and the zero brightness plane intersect.

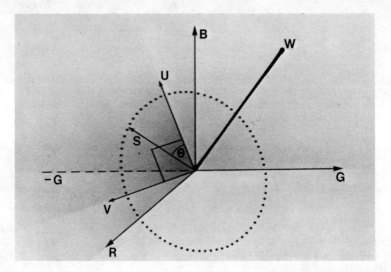

There is exactly one way of satisfying the requirement that these two lines of intersection be at right angles, and these are the two directions chosen for the non-luminance, or chrominance, components, as they are called.

Remember that these two components, called U (near blue) and V lie in the plane of zero brightness but that the positive R, G, B axes are everywhere in front of this plane, which itself is at right angles to the line of 'white'.

What, then do U and V measure? They together completely describe what is left of any colour when the maximum amount of 'white' has been removed from it; the residual colour, so to speak.

Any [U, V] pair is a vector from the origin in this chrominance plane and the **direction** of this vector represents the **Hue** of the colour. The length of the vector represents its **saturation**.

$$H = \tan^{-1}(V/U), \quad S = \sqrt{(U^2 + V^2)}$$

One day a television company is going to produce a picture of the CIE triangle projected, not down, into [r, g] space, but 'back', onto chrominance space. At present, this display is only available on the TV **vectorscope**.

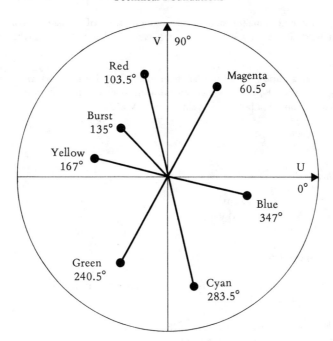

To return to the starting point of this analysis. It seems most 'natural' to specify the colour of an object in terms like Hue, Saturation and Brightness. The foregoing analysis has given some substance to the notions of these terms, and how they might relate to the quantities required by the display device, namely the values of R, G and B. There is only one choice left to be made and that is the answer to the question what is 'white'.

This is a very vexed question. At base, it is a question about the relationship of the response of the eye, as a function of wavelength, to the wavelength distribution of the light-emitting device making the picture. The physiology and psychology of visual processes indicate the wide range of accommodation possible in colour vision. The 'white' of a page of a book is seen as white in both Sunlight and Tungsten light but in each case the spectral distribution of the reflected light from the page is significantly different.

This problem was first faced by the designers of 'black and white' film emulsions. A reasonable monochrome rendering of a scene requires contributions to the total brightness from all regions of the spectrum. Similarly, in 'monochrome' TV, red objects must not appear unduly black nor blue objects unduly white. (It is usually easier to record or detect blue light than red light, since blue light has intrinsically more energy to be harnessed by the photochemistry of film emulsions or the photo-electric effects in TV tubes).

The choice of 'white' can only be made subjectively and empirically. However, there are some guiding principles. Firstly, the eye is most sensitive to 'greens'. Secondly, of the two extremes, the eye is more sensitive to changes in 'flesh tones' (the red side of green) than to small differences in 'blues'. Thirdly the eye is overall more sensitive to changes in Hue than to changes in Saturation.

The need to design a system for transmitting colour television that was compatible with existing monochrome receivers stimulated a great deal of work and, for TV at least, the following definition of 'brightness' has been adopted.

$$Y = 0.299R' + 0.587G' + 0.114B'$$

where Y is the brightness or **luminance**, composed from a mixture of the gamma-corrected signals R', G', B' so arranged that $R' = G' = B' = 1$ when the camera is pointed at a reference white under the required illumination.

Now that a choice of 'white' has been made (for TV at least), the translation from Hue, Saturation and Brightness to [R, G, B] is mechanical. Defining Hue and Saturation as (θ, S) and measuring θ counter clockwise from U (a blueish magenta) U and V are:

$$U = S.\cos(\theta)$$
$$V = S.\sin(\theta)$$

Together with Y, these give R', G' and B' as:

$$R' = Y \qquad\qquad + 0.140V$$
$$G' = Y - 0.394U - 0.581V$$
$$B' = Y + 2.020U$$

for $0 \leqslant Y \leqslant 1, 0 \leqslant S \leqslant 1, 0 \leqslant \theta \leqslant 2\pi$

The task of computing the required 'colour separation' images for a microfilm plotter, then, resolves itself into the tasks of

a. choosing the particular values of (θ, S, Y), and
b. defining 'white' to suit the display medium.

These choices fix the R, G and B values.

Colour Images from Video Devices

It is clear that the foregoing analysis applies *a fortiori* to video. There are, however, several points of interest.

In contrast to film emulsions, TV is an additive colour system that uses the R, G, B primaries directly. The range of colours that can be displayed depends on the choice of phosphors. The PAL and NTSC systems use slightly different phosphors and, with either system, the gamut of displayable colours is smaller than for most films. The development of a monochrome-compatible colour TV system took great advantage of the physiological fact that humans' colour resolution is much worse than their brightness resolution. It is very hard, for example, to define the boundary between two colours that are equally bright. The decomposition of a colour signal into [Y, U, V] meant that all the detail could be preserved in the Y component and that the other two could be transmitted with much lower fidelity yet still be able to reconstitute an acceptable picture. This can be a significant feature in the design of frame buffers.

A framebuffer is, as previously explained, an ordered piece of computer store so designed that it can be accessed sufficiently fast to support a video line. Each element on the line is represented by a **pixel** of arbitrary length. The earliest stores had 1 bit/pixel; in modern technology 16 bits/pixel is not uncommon in expensive equipment. The question arises: how best may these bits be distributed? A first guess might be 3 x 5-bit and one spare for something else. This would hold 3 points at $2^5 = 32$ levels of resolution. These could be the R, G and B picture points. This turns out not to be a good choice. A better solution is $2^8 + 2 \times 2^4$, where the luminance is held at 256 level accuracy and U, V are held to 16 levels. A variant of this is $2^8, 2^5, 2^3$ for Y, θ, S respectively, taking advantage of the physiological fact that the eye is more sensitive to changes in Hue than in changes in Saturation. Experiments at the New York Institute of Technology have shown that an even better strategy is $[2^8, 2^8]$, $[2^8, 2^8]$ holding, in adjacent pixels, $[Y_1, U_1]$, $[Y_2, V_2]$. This requires some extra hardware to hold the preceding U or V to make up the triples $[Y_n, U_n, V_{n-1}]$, $[Y_{n+1}, U_n.V_{n+1}]$ etc.

In ways such as this, the digital frame buffer can store data economically to an accuracy greater than the final display device, the 3-phosphor shadow-mask TV tube, is capable of displaying it.

THE VIDEO RASTER

The way the frame buffer is matched to the video raster is important. The PAL raster must have 768 x 575 pixels if the individual pixels are square. Broadcast PAL TV does not have square pixels in theory, although they are effectively square in practice. The reason for this is that, in the early days at least, the full visible resolution of 575 lines per picture height could not be obtained. Errors in the scanning position of both the camera and display raster, together with the effect of spot size of both the scanning and displaying beams serve to reduce the effective resolution by a factor of ~0.7, the **Kell Factor**. This gives an 'effective pixel' array of 403 x 537 square elements. A line of these elements, displayed in 52 μs, requires a bandwidth of 5.2 MHz. The bandwidth allocated to a broadcast PAL signal allows 5.5 MHz for the vision component. This bandwidth corresponds to 572 pixels per line, so the frame buffer that matches a PAL signal closely is a square array of 575 by 575 elements, each pixel having an aspect ratio of 4 x 3.

A common compromise has been to use a binary block of 512 x 512 elements. This has two major disadvantages.

1. There are not enough lines to fill the frame
2. There are two few pixels for a line of optimum resolution.

If the remaining 63 lines are added in some other way and the 512 elements strung out across the length of the line, then each pixel has an aspect ratio of 3 x 2. This means that data whose pixels are inherently square, such as the datapoints from space-craft cameras, appear distorted when displayed on such a system.

Manufacturers have a bad habit of altering the voltages which set the height and width of the TV raster on the display so as to fill the screen with a 512 x 512 image. Although the image looks acceptable, it is now NON STANDARD. Since the technology of video display is so widespread and versatile, it is good practice to stick to its specification; in this way full use can be made of the various processing and recording techniques that are available. Note in passing that a very good approximation to the frame buffer required is (9 x 64) by (12 x 64).

DATA COMPRESSION FOR RASTER SYSTEMS

The chief feature of raster systems is that every point on the writing raster has to be specified. However, it is a fact that in a great many pictures, many elements along a raster line are identical. For example, in the special case where a raster is used to simulate a vector-plotting device, the pixels representing the points not contributed to by the vector lines all have the same value – the value used to denote the background. Instead of transmitting or storing all the pixel points, it is economical of space information to map the pixel space into another domain that represents the scan line by a string of pairs of numbers, one for the value of a pixel and the other for the number of adjacent pixels which contain this value. This is the technique of **Run Length Mapping**, and it works very well for scenes containing large uniform fractions of the picture space. There are two uses for the results of this mapping. The transformed data can be stored in conventional computer stores, in which case the mapped image takes up far less space than the original pixel data, or the mapped data can, if necessary, be further coded to increase the density of information and this coded data stream then transmitted to the display device along a comparatively narrow bandwidth line. In this latter case, the display device must have the built-in facility to decode the stream and transform it back to pixel space. Note that this decoding implies a delay, since a line cannot, in general, be drawn until its decoding is complete. Compression factors of between 10 and 100 have been achieved and at least one company, Three Rivers, markets a display system based on this principle.

Run length encoding is very inefficient when there are very few identical adjacent pixels on a scan line. Unfortunately, this is the condition of images that contain a lot of information. For these images, data compression can be achieved by reducing the number of bits used to specify a pixel. This can often be achieved by **Difference Mapping**. In this technique, only the difference between successive pixels is retained after the first pixel. If the picture contains information that is varying smoothly across the scan line, then, on average, the number of bits required to specify these differences will be smaller than those required to store each individual pixel magnitude. These differences can be coded and stored or transmitted. The coding of data is a subject in itself and, where immense volumes of digital data are generated, as in satellite imagery, the techniques so far developed have a very important role to play. There is a good introduction to the subject in **Digital Image Processing** by Gonzalez and Wintz.

Character-generator Systems

The data-rates required to sustain a video raster are, as shown previously, very high in comparison with 'normal' computer data transfer rates. A popular system that reduces the data rate significantly, and emulates a teletype, is the character generator display. The central concept is to allow one data word to define one displayable character. Just as one blow on the appropriate key of a typewriter results in all the necessary marks being made on the paper to portray the chosen symbol, so the bits in one data word address a character generator that writes the entire character at the required location.

There are both vector and raster character generators and there are usually up to $2^7 = 128$ different characters available. This number is convenient for the serial transmission of data as a conventional 10-bit word composed of a 'start' bit, the 7 character bits, a parity bit and the 'stop' bit.

There is an internationally agreed, but not yet internationally accepted, correspondence between bit patterns and the set of alphanumeric characters, the ASCII code set. The appearance of the characters is determined by the character generator. Although the vector system can give a wide range of fonts, the raster-based character generators are becoming the most commonly encountered, especially the Visual Display Units (VDUs).

The technique used in raster generators is to divide the raster up into a suitable number of elementary cells, typically 24 lines of 80 character spaces, and to specify each character space by a matrix of 8 points wide and 10 points high. In raster terms this is 240 lines each containing 640 points. This corresponds exactly to the visible area of one **field** of an NTSC raster. For the PAL raster the same character positions can be specified by 9 x 12 or 10 x 11 points.

Since the complete TV picture is two interlaced fields, the simplest thing to do is repeat the same field twice. This means that each character space in the NTSC system is 20 scan lines high and 8 equivalent spaces wide.

Since the characters have to be separated from each other, there are 7 pairs of lines vertically and 5 points horizontally for each character. This is just enough to draw a capital 'E', which requires 2 horizontals and at least 2 line-pair spaces.

The dot patterns corresponding to each character code must be available on a line-by-line basis since the characters are displayed as a raster. This only requires that the Read Only Memory (ROM) in which the recipe for each character is stored be so configured as to give out the appropriate '1' or '0' for each line of the character.

The economy here is considerable. Only 24 x 80 = 1920 bytes are needed to address the whole of the screen. These bytes must arrive in 1 field period of 1/60 sec (NTSC), that is 96,000 bytes/sec, if the whole field is to be continuously updated at video rates. This is, of course not necessary. The use of an identical picture for lace and interlace requires that the 1920 characters defining the screen are be retained in a 'screen memory' for at least one field period. Since this screen memory is continuously being scanned at the video raster rate it acts like a frame buffer. Characters appear on the screen as they are written into this memory.

There is a considerable price to be paid for this economy in the data rate. The pictures are 1-bit images and only a small fraction of the screen is directly accessible.

There are other, hidden, disadvantages. Most manufacturers take very little care to see that the video raster is correctly formatted. It is extremely rare to find the interlace properly constructed and the line and field blanking periods are not often those specified by the CCIR.

A good test of the care and attention paid to raster design is to see if the VDU has a 'sync in' connecter, in addition to one labelled 'video out'. If it has, and the scanning raster can be locked to incoming video signals, the raster will have been carefully and properly designed.

Although these irregularities in the video signal are not serious from the point of view of the display, since TV monitors are, by and large, tolerant to poor synchrony, they are much more serious if the video signal has to be recorded on a videotape machine or combined with other video sources. Again, it pays in the long run to be compatible with standard video. A specification for the PAL system can be found in the IBA Technical Review No. 2 and for the NTSC system from ITU Geneva.

Teletext Systems

The video raster has 50 lines per frame that are not used for transmitting picture information. By international agreement, two of these lines per field are now set aside for the transmission of digital data. This data is used to construct rather simple images from a character generator built into the receiver. There is room on each line for 40 8-bit character words, so this system gives a data rate of 4000 characters/sec.

Once television receivers have this facility to decode a character stream built into them, they can serve as a VDU. Together with a keyboard and a telephone connection to a computer, the domestic TV receiver then becomes the home computer. The impact of this development is hard to foresee. It will put enormous strains on any telephone network that chooses to offer such a service, not least because, at least in the early stages, connection time to a computer will be longer on average than a person to person call.

Bandwidth and Signal/Noise Ratio in Electronic Systems

The two most commonly quoted measures of performance of electronic equipment are the bandwidth and the signal-to-noise ratio. From the point of view of display systems, these quantities represent measures of the spatial and grey-scale resolutions respectively. For example, by limiting the bandwidth of PAL TV to 5.5 MHz, images requiring more than about 575 pixels per line cannot be faithfully reproduced. This is because the highest frequency transmitted accurately, 5.5 MHz, is sufficient to trace out only 286 cycles in the 52 μ sec active line time.

Since this frequency is accurately reproduced, the sampling theorem requires that data at twice this rate be provided, that is, 572 pixels per line. In all encoded colour video systems, the band-width of the two chrominance components is very much reduced in comparison with the luminance. Typical values are $\sim$ 1 MHz, so that the colour is 'smeared out' over the luminance. The S/N ratio is a measure of how precisely the smallest difference in a signal can be specified. For example, if the value of a pixel is specified by 8 bits, each of the 256 levels should be resolvable. The worst case is recognising a 1 bit change in the least significant bit, so the disturbance, or noise, should be smaller than 1/256th of the signal. This ratio is usually expressed in decibels:

$$\text{S/N ratio} = -10 \log\left(\frac{1/256}{1}\right)^2 \text{ dB}$$

$$\simeq 48 \text{ dB}$$

Thus a signal to noise ratio of $>$ 50 dB is required in all parts of a system able to utilise a wordlength of 8 bits. Brightness levels of less than 8 bits (256 levels) cause unpleasant 'contouring' on surfaces where the rate of change of brightness is slow. This defect is often referred to as quantising error.

INTERACTIVE IMAGEMAKING

It is possible to divide the images produced by computation into two classes according to their mathematical nature. Some images are inherently mathematical, or can, with only a small degree of approximation, be made so. Others are not; they have no simple underlying mathematical necessity that facilitates computation. An example of this latter group might be a cartoon animation of Mickey Mouse. The shape of the figure and the motions it makes owe far more to art than science. On the other hand, an architectural drawing or a circuit diagram can be composed and defined by simple mathematical ele-ments. (At present, this seems to have produced far better circuits than buildings).

Since the only necessity in the formulation of the non-mathematical images is artistic, their construction cannot be programmed. A designer must be able to interact with the system to effect change. Even the initial data input needs to be controlled by the image designer and these requirements have fostered the development of raster-based refresh displays.

But it is not only the non-mathematical images that require the continuous intervention of the designer for their creation.

The advent of computer imagemaking has opened up a new kind of mathematical prob-lem   solving. Before the age of high-speed computation, the concept of **solution** to a mathematical problem often meant that some analytic expression has been obtained which expressed the behaviour of the system as a function of the significant variables. Making an image of this solution was straightforward and ideally suited to the batch-mode operation of early computer systems. The trouble is that only a few of the interesting problems at present have useful analytic solutions. The only way to tackle the remain-ing majority of problems is 'numerically', that is to say by formulating a suitable mathematical model and working out its consequences for a large number of choices for the values of the important variables. In some cases, the form of the final state can be specified mathematically, and so iterative minimisation procedures can be used automatically to compute the best values of the input parameters. Examples of this kind of problem are the calculations of stresses and strains in a structure such that no individual component is strained beyond its safety margin. Here again, there is no real need to intervene and a final image can be prepared at the end of the computation.

The need for interaction arises when the constraints on the problem become too difficult to compute or to express mathematically at all, even though the model of the system is itself still mathe-matical.

The design of a car body is a good example of this problem. The aerodynamic consequences of any particular shape can be computed, but the chosen final shape represents artistic choices, as well as structural and economic ones, and these are impossible to specify as targets for automatic minimisation. If a designer can watch the consequences of his artistic decisions, this component can very effectively be taken into the minimisation procedure.

There are many cases, like the course taken by a long protein molecule as it folds up into its biologically significant shape, in which classical minimisation procedures won't work and statistical methods take too long to compute. The ability to sit at a computer display and 'fold up' a long protein, choosing at every stage between alternatives dictated by the values of significant parameters, will be a very exciting and efficient way of studying protein biology. The requirements of an interactive system suitable for engineering and scientific problems is discussed by Professor Hazony in Chapter 6.

There is a third kind of interactive imagemaking that is now coming into being. This is based on the need for the **intellectual zoom**. In these problems, the task is to range through a data base representing some organisation or system. Take for example the mimic diagrams for a power transmission system. At present, the status of the system is displayed on a very large board where colour-coded lights indicate the status of the critical control points in the network. As systems increase in complexity, more and more of the routine management of the network is being taken over by computer control and some way must be found to monitor the network under these circumstances. The operator in charge must be able to 'see' the overall status of the system and be able quickly to examine in detail a particular part of the network that may need his overriding management. If the status of the system is to be displayed to the operator on some kind of TV screen, how can sufficient detail be included?

This question has led to the quest for the 'high resolution TV tube'. The trouble is that this is the wrong solution to the problem. With huge effort, tube manufacturers have been able to control the stability of the three separate image rasters and refine the shadow-mask and not quite double the maximum available horizontal resolution. By increasing the number of scan lines in the raster it is possible to attempt the display of 1024 x 1024 elements with some hope of success. In terms of this class of problem, such resolution will never be enough. The real solution lies in subtle data base management.

The fundamental structure of the problem must be embodied into the data base so that the system can be displayed in a hierarchy of levels of appropriate detail. Rather than a magnification of scale, a 'zoom' through this data base reveals more and more appropriate detail. Pioneering work of this kind has been carried out by Professor Negroponte's group at the Massachusetts Institute of Technology, although the projects that they have so far reported are of a more general nature.

TEMPORAL SEQUENCES

Interactive imagemaking plays a very important part in the analysis and understanding of systems in which the time dimension is inherent. It is also important when the time dimension is used to embody conceptual continuity. Examples of the first type of system are studies of wave motion, traffic flow, diffusion and, a particularly interesting case, atmospheric structure analysis. An example of the second kind of system is the need continually to rotate the image of a three-dimensional structure to prevent it becoming a visually ambiguous figure.

In both these cases it is useful to be able to see a succession of images interactively. This places very severe loads on both computation and display but, using a 'backing store' for the display that can cycle through a sequence of images and be written to at the line or pixel level, this can sometimes be implemented satisfactorily. If video raster technology is being used, then the analogue video disc, particularly if it is line- rather than field-addressible, can be a very versatile backing store. For 10 seconds of smooth continuous motion a minimum of 125 new images are required. This requires an analogue disc with 250 separate tracks if each track is used for one encoded colour video field or three times that number if the R, G and B components are held separately.

For digital storage, an enormous amount of store is required if no data compression is used. However, the eye is more tolerant to low-resolution pictures if they are part of a sequence displaying motion. It is as if the feature-detection systems at work in the eye-brain mechanism smooth out the image as part of the process of perceiving its contents. Thus images held as 'stills' at $512 \times 512 \times 2^8$ resolution may survive as a movie loop if carefully averaged down to $128 \times 128 \times 2^8$. Since 16 images of this reduced spatial resolution fit into the original data space for 1 image, 8 frame stores of this size will suffice for the movie loop. If these stores can be addressed fast enough with the appropriate data, this technique can be very valuable.

IMAGE PROCESSING

A great deal is already known about image processing. Because of its scientific and military importance it has attracted a good deal of attention. The mathematical foundation of the subject is secure and systems have been implemented using large main-frame computers to process data from telescopes and scanners aboard satellites. The volume of data so far collected is enormous. Images of Earth from a METEOSAT satellite arrive at the rate of three each half hour. Each of these images is a view of the Earth through a different spectral filter and has some $3,500 \times 2,500$ 8-bit pixels, or 8.75 MBy, per image.

Images of this size cannot be treated as a whole in a computer and so most image processing systems work on one line at a time. Image display has to wait for all the lines of an image to be computed. Some kind of frame buffer is required to make up for the slow speed of computation and transmission in relation to the rates required for display. Recently, however, there has been a new development that is a radical revision of this strategy. It is referred to as **pipe-line processing**.

There are two factors which have made this new development worthwhile. The first is the development of the frame buffer, in which a section of digital store is so arranged that a given sequence of pixels can be accessed at video rates to give a data stream which is fast enough to supply a video line after digital to analogue conversion. The second factor is that the majority of image-processing computations take place between nearest neighbours. For example, the Fourier Transform, required for spatial filtering and pattern recognition, is the weighted sum of successive elements along a scan line.

Since this stream of successive elements is just that which is required for the display, if a way could be found to take each one, weight it appropriately and accumulate it into a sum 'on the fly', the majority of the Fourier Transform calculations could be done at very high speed.

A very great deal of effort is expended in the design of modern computers to make the memory **appear** isotropic. The user is often unaware of where in the system, e.g. in core, on disc or even on tape, his data resides. This apparent homogenity of the address space is achieved at a cost in terms of the average time taken for an address contents to be fetched to the arithmetic unit. This design, ideal for general purpose computers, is entirely inappropriate for image processing, where there is a great deal of association between one address and the next if they form part of a store holding an image. Taken over all, the idea that in image processing, the computations on an image should be separate from its display is a bad one. Since any digital image display system, if it is raster-based, will require a piece of digital store especially designed to support the display device, the high speed of addressing (1 pixel every 68 μs for PAL) required for this display should be put to good advantage. This has been done by companies such as the Stanford Technology Corporation in their $I^2 S$ image processing system.

A typical image processing system of this type will have several stores, often each $512 \times 512 \times 8$, so arranged that the digital data stream from each store can be generated simultaneously and combined, element by element along a line, in several different ways simultaneously to give a number of outputs, often 3, which can be used to drive the R, G and B inputs of a colour TV monitor.

Suppose for example, that there are 3 stores, each containing the same part of a meteosat image of Earth through a different spectral filter. By judicious choices of the combinations of each pixel intensity summed to the R, G and B inputs, the resulting false colour image might show the different types of cloud present in the image giving each cloud a different colour. By means of data from the Landsat satellites, this technique, using images from 5 or more spectral bands, it is possible to identify and colour-code differences as subtle as the ripeness of crops.

Colour, False Colour and Pseudo-Colour

Coloured images are more appealing than monochrome images. Features not readily appa-rent in a monochrome image become more noticable when they are arbitrarily coloured. There are also a whole class of images for which colour has no meaning, for example the images from a CAT brain scan or body scan. In these cases the data is the relative opacity to X-rays of a particular region in the object. Rather than display these densities as a greyscale, it is sometimes more striking to transform these pixel values into a sequence of colours. This technique, where a greyscale image is arbitrarily assigned to some colour value, is called **pseudo-colour imaging**. A very common palette for pseudo-colour pictures contains the eight possible colours available if R, G and B can have only the values 0 or 1. They are:

R	G	B	Result	Y	Grey level	Assignment range	γ-Corrected assignments ($\gamma = 1/2.2$)
0	0	0	Black	0.00	0	0 - 13	0 - 46
0	0	0	Blue	0.11	28	14 - 51	47 - 120
1	0	0	Red	0.30	77	52 - 90	121 - 159
1	0	1	Magenta	0.41	105	91 - 127	160 - 185
0	1	0	Green	0.59	151	128 - 164	186 - 209
0	1	1	Cyan	0.70	180	165 - 203	210 - 229
1	1	0	Yellow	0.89	228	204 - 241	230 - 248
1	1	1	White	1.0	256	242 - 256	249 - 255

In this table the R, G, B combinations are arranged in their order of TV luminance (this is the order of the 'colour bars' used as test transmissions for television). This suggests a possible mapping. All pixel values between 0 and 13 (assuming 256 levels are available) could be assigned to 'black', levels between 14 and 51 to blue, levels 52 to 90 for red and so on, white being represented by any of the pixel values bet-ween 242 and 256. The last column represents the assignments gamma-corrected for a typical colour TV display.

There is a very quick device for making such transformations that has come to have great application in digital imagemaking: it is called the **Look-up table** (LUT). It is nothing more than a small piece of digital store so arranged that if it is addressed by the bits representing the pixel **value** the con-tents of that address is the desired transform value.

Thus, in this example, for the uncorrected case, the first 14 locations of the look-up table would contain the bit pattern 000, the next 38 locations the bit pattern 001, the next 40 the pattern 100 and so on. This transformed data stream, which is travelling just as fast in the pipeline as the original pixel data since this address look-up can be very fast indeed, can be interpreted in a very simple manner to drive the separate R, G and B channels as required by the bit patterns.

Some idea of the flexibility and versatility of this sytem can be appreciated by realising that it is easily possible to load the 256 values into the look-up table during the TV field interval. This means that the colours of a 'monochrome' image can be varied just as fast as they can be computed, by whatever rule, and loaded into the look-up table. Using this technique Dick Shoup has devised some very simple yet effective video animation techniques. This kind of transformation is the simplest use of look-up tables in the generation of pseudo-colour images. The next level of complexity might be to use three LUTs, each with a different map, and each dedicated to a particular R, G or B channel. These can be addressed by the same pixel value to give a very wide range of colour and brightness assignments. Moreover, these assignments can be changed interactively to choose a visually acceptable result. All in all it is a very powerful technique.

The other two types of coloured image, (true) colour and false colour, refer to the generation of a coloured image from more than one distinct pixel array. **True colour images** are those which result from the combination of 3 images whose pixel values correspond to the brightnesses required by the colours of the display device. All other multi-image combinations are **false colour images**. For example, the spectral filters in the visible region on the telescopes of the Voyager Spacecraft are an orange red, a blue green, a blue and a violet. They were not chosen to match the phosphors of a TV tube but rather for the scientific information they might yield. Thus there is no combination that gives 'true colour'. The definition of white as $(0.3R' + 0.59G' + 0.11B')$ does not apply in this case.

Look-up Tables in the Pipeline

The look-up table is a very valuable device. If the outputs of two frame stores each pass through look-up tables, where the contents of the address is the **logarithm** of the address, before being summed, and the sum passes through a look-up table whose contents are the anti-logarithm of the address, the result is the **product** of corresponding pixel pairs in the two framestores. The word-length of the look-up tables must be such that not too much accuracy is lost in the process. Nevertheless, it is a much faster way of multiplying two numbers than the conventional floating-point multiplier. In this way, in one frametime, two 512 x 512 x 8 images can be multiplied or ratioed point by point: this is more than 6.5 million 8-bit multiplications or divisions per second. Performing this operation by conventional processing would be very slow indeed by comparison, with most of the time being spent looking for each number to multiply or divide. Perhaps the simplest use of a look-up table is to transform the contrast range of an image; a digital gamma-corrector, so to speak.

Computations on the Image Address Space

So far the image has always been considered as being fixed, and display as taking place by reading set locations out in order. If, instead of starting at the point corresponding to the top left hand corner of the image, the reading out starts at the centre of the picture, it is easy to arrange the computing of the addresses to be fetched for display so that a whole line for display is formed from the second half of one line and the first half of the adjacent line. This has the effect of scrolling the picture diagonally upwards or downwards. It is also easy to arrange that other picture memories be incorporated into this display. In this way 16 framestores could be linked together to hold a 2048 x 2048 image (almost all of a METEOSAT image) and a 512 x 512 display window could be 'rolled' across this large image just displaying the portion in the window, simply by recomputing the starting address for the display.

These are only hints as to the range of processing power available on such systems as the Micro Consultants' **Intellect** system.

Television Applications of Frame Store Technology

It is only recently that computer display manufacturers have begun to take account of the exact TV formats. One company, Quantel Limited, has specialised in developing digital display processors that operate in real time on the stored video signal. Once a frame of video is 'frozen' into a store, it is possible to average values of adjacent pixels to produce a new image that is larger, smaller or shifted in relation to the original. The parameters governing the distortion can be controlled by potentio-meters whose values are sampled sufficiently often to compute a sequence of distortions on the incoming video data stream that gives rise to a smooth development of the distortion. For example, an incoming TV image can be shrunk and repositioned within the frame in real time, ready to be inserted into a second video image by some electronic technique such as Chromakey (CSO).

Other Video Techniques

Digital methods are not the only ones to be employed in the manipulation of video images. Analogue techniques that modify the raster shape have been employed for a number of years with great success. **Image West** in Hollywood have produced a large amount of high-quality animation for both film and video use and have set a style and standard for the digital systems to live up to. These systems are inherently 2-D and so any appearance of depth is purely artistic; however, some of the effects are visually interesting and have become part of the vocabulary of computer animation. A full description of this type of equipment, by Ed Tajchman, can be found in Chapter 5.

COMPUTATIONAL STRATEGIES

In Chapter 3 DeFanti and Sandin use a memorable metaphor; they talk of the 'software swamp'. Much of the problem derives from the fact that so far, no-one has discovered the natural lang-uage for imagemaking. Computation is in a transition phase at present. There are still essentially two modes of access to computing facilities, the **Batch** mode and the **Interactive** mode. The foregoing para-graphs have indicated the relevance of the interactive mode of computation to a wide range of computer imagemaking. The trouble is that quite a lot of 'interactive environments' are, more accurately, 'botch batch', where the old system has been 'fixed' to make it appear as if the system is running interactively. In an ideal world, the concept of batch processing as a separate style must disappear — a batch job is just an interactive job with no interaction.

The developments in the theory of computer language in recent years augur well for the coming of a language whose syntax is ideally suited to image formation and manipulation. It will almost certainly be an interpretive, rather than a compiled language, and the groundwork for its form is being explored by such groups as the GRIP and CORE projects. An interesting discussion of the various lang-uages and their merits as vehicles for image construction can be found in **Interactive Computer Graphics** by W.K. Giloi.

CREATING REALISTIC IMAGES

There are a great many visual cues that help in the deciphering of an image. If an image is a representation of a three-dimensional scene, then all the devices of perspective can be used to give structure to the image. However, these devices are often nullified if the objects in the space do not behave properly. We are not accustomed to seeing a view composed of transparent objects. Perhaps the over-riding feature of our visual field is occlusion. The way in which objects in the scene hide each other is the most powerful cue to depth. This raises one of the most engaging problems of seeing — what is the smallest amount of visual information necessary to infer correctly the form of the hidden part of an object, and how does this information depend on the nature of the object being analysed. When we have answers to these questions, perhaps it will be possible to design the perfect image-making computer. In the meantime, ways have been found satisfactorily to simulate the occlusion of one computed object by another. This is called the **Hidden Surface problem**, and there are several solutions known so far.

They fall into two main types, those in which the tests for visibility are performed in the object space and those in which the test is performed in the image space. However, both depend on the method used to represent the object. In all cases the 'object' is specified by its surfaces and these surfaces are defined mathematically. One of the most widely used systems is to divide the surface up into the smallest possible number of plane polyhedrons. Figures with 3, 4, 5 and 6 sides have been used singly or together and the technique is an extension of the idea of representing a circle by a number of chords. This procedure generates a 'wireframe' model of the object and this can be represented as a list of [x,y,z] triples, one for each point, and a list showing which point joins to what others. Using the techniques of Algebraic and Differential geometry, the planes can be identified, their lines of intersection with each other and with the limit of the visible picture determined and, by examining the direction of each normal, whether or not the plane is facing the eye and is visible. The result of this kind of analysis is a list of [X,Y] pairs and a new list of their interconnections. These are the lines to be drawn by the vector plotting device. This system gives wireframe images with the hidden lines removed.

Instead of decomposing the figure into polyhedrons, where the 'fixed points' are joined by straight lines, it is often better to use **spline functions**. These functions are 'piecewire continuous' polynomials, so, for example, the polygon is a spline function of order 1; the polynomials joining the points are of order 1, i.e. lines. Higher order splines can fit arbitrary points, or 'knots' as they are referred to in the theory, very smoothly without many of the unwanted properties of a single polynomial passing through the same points.

The value of these approximations, which can be generalised to 2-D 'patches' is that they define the surface of the object 'everywhere', instead of just at the original grid-points. This means that the object may quite easily be 'rasterised' by finding the points where a 'ray' from a pixel to the eye intersects the surface(s). Furthermore, since the functions are analytic, the normal to the surface at that intersection can always be calculated. The division of the original object into a minimum number of patches of a specialised form, e.g. bi-quadrate or bi-cubic, is a matter of judgement; thereafter the fitting and blending of the patches can proceed automatically. An excellent review of the various techniques can be found in **Interactive Computer Graphics** by W. K. Giloi and in **Tutorial of Computer Graphics** ed. K. S. Booth.

Perhaps the next most powerful cue to structure and form in an image is the effect of light and shade. We rarely see the world in perfectly uniform illumination. The shadows cast by the sun, or the principal light on a scene, give an orientation that we have learnt to make good use of. Much of the most recent work in computer graphics has been directed at this problem.

The patterns of light and shade on an object are the result not only of the light source but also of the nature of the reflecting surface. Surface reflections are of two kinds; mirror-like reflections, in which the angles of incidence and reflection are equal, and scattering, where the incident light is diffused out in all directions from the surface. This latter kind arises from the absorption and re-emission of the incident light by the surface and hence the properties of the surface are represented in the re-emitted light; this is the light that is 'coloured' after falling on an object. Apparently red objects, for example, have absorbed more blue and green light than red light from the incident radiation, so that the light reaching the eye contains a higher proportion of red wavelengths than the incident radiation. The mirror-like or **specular** reflections do not behave in this way. They have instead, all the properties of the light source. The exact reproduction of the total reflectance of a surface is the combination of these two types; moreover, the precise forms of both the specular and scattered components depends on the nature of the surface. Various mathematical models have been devised which represent very well the behaviour of a range of surfaces, and the characterisation of many surfaces is accomplished now by specifying one or two parameters in a simple mathematical function.

In all these models, the computations depend on a knowledge of three directions: the direction of the light source from the surface, the direction of the viewing point and the direction of the normal to the surface, all at the point where the intensity of the reflected light must be calculated. All the recent techniques for generating surfaces have a method for computing the normal at a picture point. The intensity calculations are not difficult, just very long in comparison with all the other steps in generating the surface, particularly if there are several light sources.

The images produced to date using the best models for illumination have a strange failing. They are too perfect. This is particularly true of 'metallic' surfaces, where the specular component dominates the scattered component. These images lack a fundamental property of real objects: **surface texture**. One of the triumphs of the most recent work in computer imaging has been the simulation of surface texture by **texture mapping**.

The texture of a surface can be modelled by giving the surface three-dimensional undulations. This is prohibitively expensive in computer time and, in any case, is not a good solution, since all it would lead to is a different value for the surface normal at each point. By devising a way systematically to 'nudge' the existing surface normals slightly in a range of directions, exactly the same effect can be achieved at a fraction of the computational effort.

Using this technique, Jim Blinn has achieved remarkable results. A detailed treatment of the raster scan techniques that are currently in use for the simulations of reality can be found in his PhD thesis for the University of Utah, Department of Computer Science 1978.

In the world in which we live, there is a third method for decoding our image of the world: **Stereopsis**. Our two eyes give us slightly different view of the world and the retinal disparities between perceived objects gives a cue to distance that is very powerful.

There have been many attempts to simulate stereopsis on film and television. To date the most promising methods are based on the reciprocal polarisation of the views destined for each eye, so that, by viewing a scene through appropriately polarising glasses, each eye can be given only the view it should see. There is an even older technique that works for both printing and projected images, and that is the **anaglyph** system. Here, the image separation is achieved by drawing each eye's view in a different colour and viewing the scene through glasses that filter out the unwanted colour at each eye. Using the red/green anaglyph system, I have been able to present acceptable stereo pictures of vector-drawn ball and-stick images of the haemoglobin molecule. The great advantage of this stereoscopic technique is that it eliminates the need for any 'hidden line' calculations and so the large numbers of frames required for a 25 minute 3-D movie, showing sometimes up to 800 atom-bond pairs at a time, can be computed without undue expense.

SUMMARY

Computer imagemaking has, over the last twenty years, become a worthwhile activity. Although still limited by technology, the range and versatility of computed images is now such that few everyday activities cannot benefit from their use. A large number of fundamental theoretical problems have been solved, such as the hidden surface problem, and in the next decade, computer-produced images will become steadily more 'painterly'. High quality images will continue to be produced on microfilm recorders but more and more effort will be devoted to high-speed video processing and display. The annual meetings of the Special Interest Group in graphics (SIGGRAPH) of the Association for Computing Machinery will continue to be the major international forum for the exchange of information.

When we 'see', the first stage of that process is to reduce the 3-D world to a 2-D world on our retinas. If the object of interest is **already** a 2-D model of a 3-D world, we must expect that ambiguities may arise in the interpretation of the object. The fewer the number of artifacts introduced by the display technology into this 2-D object the better. Good design of images for display, that takes account, not only of inherent defects in the visual system but also of fundamental limitations in the technology of computation and display, will result in effective, viewable images that justify the old expression: a picture is worth a thousand words.

This is a Mercator projection, computed by Dr R. Saunders, of the METEOSAT image facing page one. The polar regions are omitted but the data for Northern Europe is still rich enough to be expanded still further to give good dynamic weather maps for this part of the world.

SEEING HYPOTHESES

Richard L. Gregory
Brain & Perception Laboratory
University of Bristol

The Human Visual System is not yet understood. Good as it is, it is nevertheless prone to error. We draw the wrong conclusions from what we see. These illusions are interesting because they may reveal the mechanisms of perception. In designing 2-D images, the factors which promote illusion must be understood if ambiguous figures are not to be drawn by accident.

INTRODUCTION

It is clear from physiology that perception depends upon neural signals, trains of action potentials, from the organs of sense. The sense organs are essentially like the detecting instruments of physics and engineering: transducers transforming selected patterns of energy into signals from which external events may be read. It seems perception is like science, in using sensory signals to select and test hypotheses of the external world. If so, perceptions are but indirectly related to the world — related by signals and steps of inference.

The principal founder of the modern experimental study of perception, Hermann von Helmholtz (1821 - 1894), was concerned to discover physiological mechanisms of the eye, the ear, and the other organs of sense and the nervous system; but he did not believe that a description of these mechanisms would give a complete description of perception. He held that the central nervous system must be carrying out 'unconscious inferences' to make effective use of the sensory signals (Ref. 1). Why did Helmholtz, who was a great physiologist, reject the 'straightforward' physiological account that perception is given directly by signals? Why did he hold that elaborate inferences are necessary for perception? It is particularly interesting that he did so before the impact of computers on our appreciation of the power of inference outside the formal proofs of mathematics and the idealized system of physics. A vital reason is the simple fact (often ignored) that the senses cannot continuously provide adequate and relevant signals — which would be necessary for direct control of behaviour or perception. Behaviour follows assumptions, such as that a chair has four legs, though one or more are hidden; or that a table is strong, though the eyes cannot test its strength — and behaviour continues through data gaps, as we turn away or objects pass out of sight.

THEORIES OF PERCEPTION

The most generally held account of perception which is still frequently defended by philosophers, is that perception is direct knowledge. It is held today by the distinguished psychologist

James J. Gibson, who holds that perception is passive 'pick-up of information from the ambient array of light' and that what we see is determined by stimulus patterns, such as texture gradients and by motion parallax as we move. To cartoon the 'straightforward' physiological account: perceptions are held to be made of neural signals.

On Helmholtz's account perceptions are conclusions of inferences. He urged that to understand perception it is just as important to appreciate the procedures of inference as it is to understand the physiological processes of signal transmission by the nervous system. Helmholtz's Unconscious Inference has however been strongly resisted: initially because inference was associated with conscious processes, and awareness of the steps was supposedly necessary; and perhaps now – in spite of the obvious power of computers to carry out inferences without consciousness – the dramatic success of physiology in revealing mechanisms by which neural signals are transmitted and handled makes 'strategy' or 'cognitive' accounts seem pallid and vague by comparison. This is, however, beginning to change, with growing success and awareness of picture-processing procedures.

Some distinguished physiologists do however still hold that further elucidation of neural mechanisms will provide the whole story, so that cognitive concepts will fade out as unnecessary. This is to say that electronics is all we need to know about computers. Programmers, however, take a very different view – essentially Helmholtz's view – that we must appreciate procedures independently of our understanding of mechanisms carrying out the procedures. They would deny that 'software' accounts can be reduced to 'hardware' accounts, and would hold that procedures (or cognitive processes) can be considered quite apart from any mechanisms in which they may be embodied.

Broadly speaking, there are three rival paradigms of perception.

1. The direct or 'intuitive' knowledge, as held by Bishop Berkeley in the Eighteenth Century and by James J. Gibson today (Refs. 2,3).

2. The sense organs are regarded as transducers, providing neural signals which are supposed, somehow, to add up to perceptions.

3. Perceptions are inferences from stored and currently available signalled data. This is essentially Helmholtz's view, that perceptions are still more indirectly related to the world than implied in paradigm 2.

In the first paradigm perceptions are selections of the world, and so direct knowledge, while in the second paradigm perceptions are patterns of neural signals derived from the world via the sense organ transducers. On the second paradigm perception is not direct, and is open to errors through malfunctioning of the transducers and the mechanisms of the signal channels. On the third paradigm there is no simple one-to-one relation between neural activity and perceptual phenomena (which is another reason why it is none too popular with physiologists). On this paradigm perceptions are extrapolations from available data, and are generally much richer than the data.

I like to think of perceptions as 'hypotheses' – essentially like the predictive hypotheses of physics (Ref.4). Both make effective use of limited signals or data, to predict and control events of the environment. Both make use of knowledge derived from the past to predict and control the future. Both depend on inference. It is interesting to compare scientific hypotheses, and how they are derived, with perceptions in rather more detail.

Visual illusions take on a deep theoretical significance if perceptions are hypotheses, and it is also instructive to compare the properties of scientific hypotheses and perceptions to see how illusions might arise.

A Comparison of Hypotheses with Perceptions

Signals from Transducers — Both depend on signals from transducers being processed as data. This involves selecting signals from noise, integrating and sometimes coincidence-gating to increase the signal/noise ratio; and comparing sources for discrepancies. There may be, additionally, more sophisticated procedures for accepting signals as data such as statistical significance tests. In any case, we cannot recognise signals as data without knowing the coding.

Calibration — Calibration of the transducers is necessary in both cases, and may involve subtle procedures including: (i) Comparison with signals or data from other transducers (other instruments or other organs of sense) given the same input; (ii) Comparison of current with expected signals or data (which requires stored knowledge of what to expect).

Instruments, or sense organs, may receive calibration corrections. When these are inappropriate, systematic errors (illusions) are generated, though the mechanisms may have no fault. (Thus, after adapting to distorting spectacles, the world appears distorted, in directions opposite to the original distortion).

Scaling According to Assumed Invariances — This is a kind of calibration, but involves specific assumptions about the situation in which the instrument or sensory system is being used. For example, a pilot may assume that the texture over which he is flying is roughly uniform in average density, to estimate his height and his approach path when landing — as well as assuming that the runway is parallel and the buildings square and so on. Such assumptions, though usually very useful, can generate serious problems. For example, helicopter pilots flying over oases in deserts have to be careful, for the density of the vegetation falls off regularly with distance away from the source of water: so he appears to be climbing when in fact he is approaching the ground. Distances of stars are judged by similar assumptions for setting the scaling constants, as for vision.

Entertaining Alternatives — Data is always, strictly speaking, ambiguous and may be accepted as evidence of a wide variely of alternative hypotheses. (Indeed, variety is limited only by the limitations of imagination). Perceptions can switch spontaneously between alternatives with no change of data; and much the same happens in science, especially with changes of accepted paradigm (Ref.5).

Guidance by Conditional Probabilities — Data may be accepted, rejected, or interpreted according to the likelihoods of alternative hypotheses. It is thus easier to perceive a likely than an unlikely object in a given context. But this implies (and it is not difficult to demonstrate) that unlikely objects bearing marked similarities to highly probable objects are readily confused with them, and may be impossible to recognise for what they are. For example, the hollow mold of a face appears with its nose sticking out — though it is hollow — against all manner of texture and other sensory data simply because a hollow face is so unlikely (Fig. 1). There is a similar limitation in testing unlikely scientific hypotheses: when extremely unlikely, the instrument is more likely to be in error than that the event has occurred. (Thus it would be impossible to test the prediction that, very occasionally, a pan of water will freeze when put on the gas stove — for observational error or delusion of some kind is more likely than the event, even though this is predicted as a possibility).

Handle New Cases — It is striking that we can perceive objects from unfamiliar positions, and see unusual objects — though there are limitations — and similarly, scientific hypotheses handle new cases but with limitations.

Hypotheses based on wide-ranging generalizations have great power to deal with new cases; and, where there are powerful heuristic rules, highly surprising conclusions may be derived.

Generate Fiction — Both scientific hypotheses and perceptions may lead into dramatic error — which may however suggest some new and useful solutions.

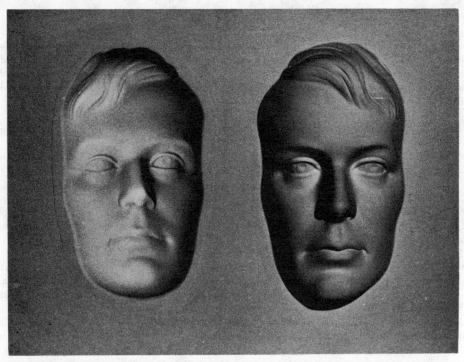

Fig. 1 The face on the right is as it appears, but the one on the left is in fact its hollow mold. A hollow face is so unlikely that texture, and even stereoscopic data signalling to the eye that it is hollow, are discounted. It is virtually impossible to present such an unlikely object vertically with any available electronic display.

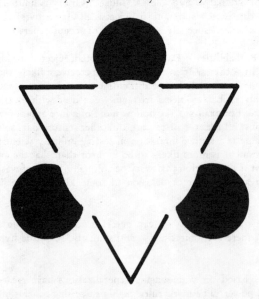

Fig. 2 This illusory white disc seems to be produced by the unlikely gaps suggesting the presence of a nearer masking object. This is evidently postulated by the visual system.

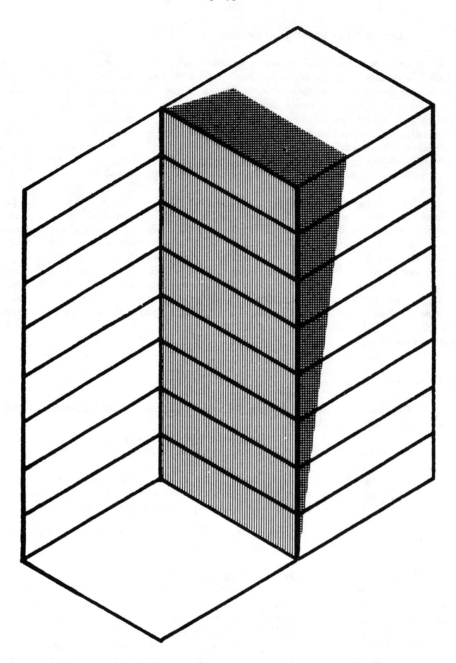

Fig. 3 This is a depth-ambiguous figure with a 'shadow'. It may be noted that the 'shadow' appears dark with one depth-orientation of the figure, and light with the other orientation. It is light when a plausible shadow, such as that cast by top lighting. We thus see 'Brightness Constancy' triggered internally by the prevailing depth-hypothesis. This is an example of 'top-down' scaling; as the stimulus pattern, or input to the eye, remains constant.

ILLUSIONS IN HUMAN PERCEPTION

Errors or illusions may be due to failure, or loss of calibration, of the transducers of the signal channel or breakdown of the computing systems – but they may also be due to inappropriateness of the hypothesis-generating procedures. Although signal distortion through mechanical or electrical trouble with the channel (including overloading and cross-talk) is extremely different, conceptually, from errors due to inappropriate procedures or from false assumptions of invariances, yet it is surprisingly difficult to distinguish in practice between physiological and cognitive errors, or illusions. I shall illustrate this by considering the classical problem of the origin of visual distortion illusions. There are, however, as well as distortion illusions, other kinds of illusions notably: Ambiguity, Paradox, and Created or Hallucinatory features such as 'cognitive contours'. Examples are shown in Figs. 2 and 3.

Distortions can clearly occur in two ways: first, 'upwards' by certain stimulus patterns (either because they disturb the signal channel or because they provide data which are inappropriate to the situation) and secondly, 'downward' from the prevailing assumption or perceptual hypothesis or relative distances or depth of the perceived objects or display. It is a most important fact that with apparent alterations of apparent depth in objects, such as occurs in 'wireframe models', the apparently further features are expanded, and shrink when the depth reverses so that they appear nearer. This shows conclusively that apparent size can be set purely by apparent distance independently of the stimulus pattern. It is thus clear that not all distortions can be due to channel characteristics, and there is at least this tie-up between apparent distance and apparent size – which is no doubt part of the scaling processes normally giving Size Constancy. If perceptual scaling giving size constancy were to be set inappropriately size distortion must result.

Size/Depth Distortion Illusions

The classical problem of the origin or cause of visual distortion illusions has at least three rival accounts worth serious consideration:

1.   neural interactions, such as lateral inhibition, or other neural channel distortions;

2.   spatial frequency characteristics of the visual system, associated with Fourier-like transforms, supposedly important for pattern recognition: low pass filter characteristics are held to produce the distortions, especially with converging lines;

3.   size scaling, set by perspective features (such as convergence) which when presented on flat picture planes gives inappropriate scaling.

It has proved surprisingly difficult to distinguish experimentally between **physiological** and more **cognitive** accounts, though the logical distinctions between these alternatives seem reasonably clear (Ref. 6). Experiments have been designed to provide evidence for or against a cognitive account, such as the Inappropriate Constancy Scaling Theory, which requires the organism to act on knowledge or assumptions of features of the object world. This theory is, unlike the alternatives mentioned above, a cognitive account because it supposes that the visual system is acting (correctly or inappropriately) from stored knowledge of characteristics of the world. The illusion is attributed to applying knowledge to situations inappropriately. The ways in which the knowledge is stored and used – the physiological mechanisms involved – need not be specified for this to be a legitimate and for many purposes adequate account. The first kind of theory, on the other hand, supposes that a modification of the physiological mechanism or channel is responsible. The second class of theory (Ref. 7) makes no such demand or claim on detailed physiological understanding; and neither does it call on cognitive processes, involving knowledge of or assumptions about external objects. The three kinds of theory are so conceptually different that the experimental difficulty of deciding between them is surprising. Perhaps this difficulty is due to the reasonable biological assumption that even peripheral mechanisms will be adapted to handle typical objects. We should therefore expect to find crucial differences only in situations requiring stored knowledge of specific classes of objects or visual features. The Inappropriate Constancy Scaling theory does refer to specific classes of features — especially converging of parallel lines by perspective. Retinal perspective (given by optical projection at the retina), used as information for depth, depends on assumptions of the sizes of objects and typical shapes especially parallel and right angular features, which hold more generally in some environments than in others. Considerable anthropological data are now available supporting the suggestion that distortion illusions are greatest for people living in 'carpentered' environments (Refs. 8, 9).

The notion that distortion illusions such as the Muller-Lyer and Ponzo figures are perspective drawings goes back at least to Thiery (Ref. 10). He did not realize that typical objects (such as outside corners of buildings, inside corners of rooms, or receding parallel lines) must be accepted as paradigm objects, to infer depth from retinal perspective. (Thiery's example of the legs of a saw horse is misleading – for the legs could be of almost any angle). Neither did he suggest a **modus operandi** relating depth features to distortion on picture planes. This was suggested by Tausch (Ref. 11) as Size Constancy; but was later rejected by him, as depth distortions occur though depth may not be seen in these figures. In Gregory (Ref. 12) I suggested that constancy can be given by size and shape scaling set directly by depth cues even though depth is not seen. This would be 'automatic', and takes place at a low level in the nervous system.

The Inappropriate Constancy Scaling theory makes a specific prediction: illusory distortions should vanish when the perspective and the perception of depth are appropriate.

To test this prediction, an experiment must be designed to **destroy** an illusion. This ability to destroy an illusion is valuable in two ways. Firstly, the ability to construct the circumstances required to remove the illusion that the mechanisms is understood. Secondly, it is useful to be able to remove illusions from displays.

The strategy of the experiment, performed by John Harris and myself (Ref. 13) was to ensure that both the 'upward' and 'downward' scalings were appropriate. By controlling the apparent depth using stereoscopic projection ('downward' scaling) and setting the perspective precisely ('upward' scaling) we were able to show that the length-distortion illusion in the Muller-Lyer figures produced by the projection of right-angular corners of 3-D wire models vanished only when the scalings were appropriate.

Feature-locking Distortion Illusions

The components of the nervous system are, by comparison with electronic components, subject to drift and are generally labile, in ways intolerable to electronic engineers. Also, the retinal receptors (the rods, and the three types of cones serving colour vision) have different time-constants, so retinal signals are variously delayed according to intensity and colour. In spite of this, regions of different colour and brightness are very seldom seen with mis-registration of borders. This is surprising, for electronic displays such as colour TV show marked discrepancies between regions of different colour or intensity, especially with motion. The integrity of TV displays depends upon the stability of the components. The nervous system has no such stability, and yet we seldom see discrepancies at borders — though even TV is prone to registration errors in spite of the high stability of its components.

This suggests that there is some special principle active in the nervous system to maintain registration at borders.

It has recently been found (Ref. 14) that brightness, colour, and movement are represented in the cerebral cortex in different cortical 'maps'. This makes the fact that registration is normally maintained within visual acuity even more surprising.

We may suppose (Ref. 15) that registration is maintained by locking signals at contrast borders. I think we can see our own locking system at work, in the illusion shown in Fig. 4a, b, c. This consists of alternating brightness-contrasting regions (squares) separated by narrow parallel lines. In (a) the intensity of the separating lines is less than the darker squares; in (b) it lies between the darker and lighter squares. In (c) it is brighter than the light squares. In the conditions (b), when the separating lines lie within the brightness range of the square, a marked distortion is seen: the parallel separating lines do not appear parallel but seem to converge alternately to form wedges. The distortion illusion is destroyed by taking the intensity of the separating lines outside the range of intensities of the alternating squares.

We find, also, that neighbouring regions of contrasting colour but the same brightness (different colours set to isoluminant match) are not positionally stable, but shift relatively with motion; and the colour-contrast border is unstable and 'jazzy'. This distortion illusion does not occur with coloured squares (red and green) when the colours have equal brightness (Ref. 15).

I suggest that colour borders (which are absent in the special case of isoluminant colours) and the positions of intensity borders, are set, within the lability of the system, by the relative intensities either side of them around isoluminance.

The illusion of Fig. 4a, b, c, (which we call the 'Cafe Wall Illusion', since we first observed it in the Victorian tiles of a cafe near our laboratory in Bristol) may be explained by supposing that the borders of the squares 'see' locking signals across the separating lines (the 'mortar'), when this has an intensity between the dark and light squares. When the 'mortar' is varied continuously, in the model from which these photographs were made, it is observed that the dark squares move toward the lighter squares while the 'mortar' is dark, and the light squares move towards the dark squares while the 'mortar' is light – within the intensity range of the dark and light squares. This would be expected with locking by intensity signals 'seen' across the separating 'mortar' lines.

This distortion does seem to be essentially different from the classical Distortion Illusions. They, if we are correct, arise from inappropriately applied knowledge of the world: especially perspective convergence normally associated with distance applied to a picture plane. Since this is flat, the scaling set by the picture perspective features is inappropriate and produces distortion. The distortion of the 'Cafe Wall Illusion', if we are correct, arises from inadequacies of the neural components of the visual channel. This has nothing to do with knowledge of the world – and so is not a cognitive illusion – while the classical perspective distortion illusions are cognitive illusions.

The first experiment illustrated **data mismatching**. Angle features of this illusion figure (and the other classical distortion illusions of this type) are evidently accepted as data for depth, which in this case is misleading, to set Size Constancy Scaling, in this case, inappropriately. This is very different from a **signal mismatch**, which depends purely on physical characteristics (such as filter characteristics) of the channel, and not at all on the significance of the message. The second experiment shows a rather special but quite dramatic example of signal mismatch when the channel distorts the retinal signals, due, we may suppose in this case, to inadequacies of neural components and mechanisms which counter these inadequacies in normal conditions.

These are just two illustrations of the ways in which images can be misleading. A clearer understanding of the factors which lead to illusory perceptions can be of great use in the design of unambiguous displays.

Fig. 4 The 'Cafe Wall'

REFERENCES

1. H. L. F. von Helmholtz, (1962) **Handbook of Physiological Optics**. Trans. 1924, Dover.

2. J. J. Gibson, (1950) **The Perception of the Visual World**, Greenwood Press, Westport, Conn.

3. J. J. Gibson, (1966) **The Senses Considered as Perceptual Systems**, Houghton Mifflin, Boston.

4. R. L. Gregory, (1970) **The Intelligent Eye**, McGraw-Hill, New York.

5. T. Kuhn, (1970) **The Structure of Scientific Revolutions**, Univ. Chicago Press.

6. R. L. Gregory, (1975) Do we need cognitive concepts? **Handbook of Psychobiology**, Blackmore and Gazzinaga (eds), Academic Press.

7. A. P. Ginsburg, Psychological correlates of a model of the human visual system, **Proc. IEEE NAEOON**, 283-390, (1971).

8. M. H. Segall, T. D. Campbell and M. J. Herskovitz, (1966) **The Influence of Culture on Visual Perception**, Bobbs Merril, New York

9. J. Deregowski, (1974) Illusion and culture. **Illusion in Nature and Art**, Gregory and Gombrich (eds), Chas. Schribner, New York.

10. A Thiery, Ueber Geometrisch-optische Tauschungen **Phil. Stud 12**, 67 (1896).

11. R. Tausch, Optische Tauschungen als artifizielle Effekte der Gestaltungsprozesse von Grossen and Formenkonstanz in der naturlichen Raumwahrnehmung. **Psychol. Forsch. 24**, 299 (1954).

12. R. L. Gregory, Distortion of visual space as inappropriate constancy scaling. **Nature 199**, 678

13. R. L. Gregory and J. P. Harris, Illusion destruction by appropriate scaling. **Perception 4**, 203-220, (1975).

14. S. M. Zecki, Colour coding in the superior temporal sulcus of rhesus monkey visual cortex. **Proc. R. Soc. Lond. B. 197**, 195-223, (1977).

15. R. L. Gregory, Vision with isoluminant colour contrast: 1. A projection technique and observations. **Perception 6**, 113-119, (1976).

MATCHING THE SYSTEM TO THE GOALS

OR

TV OR NOT TV

Tom DeFanti, Information Engineering
Dan Sandin, School of Art and Design
University of Illinois at Chicago Circle

This chapter sets out the factors that can affect the choice of method to be used to display computed images. The strengths and weaknesses of the various modes are compared and contrasted and some specific examples of systems designed to do a particular job are given. In the end, it all comes down to money; the prices mentioned are in dollars as of January 1980.

ORGANIZING PRINCIPLE OF THIS CHAPTER

The application of computers to artificial image production and manipulation requires a knowledge of the equipment available, the software techniques, and the various mechanisms for displaying and recording images. The goals must be seen as subject to the disposable time and expense, and, not to be underestimated, the available expertise. We will try to make clear the compromises that must be made when choosing between the approaches to the computer graphics systems we present. We will attempt to be exhaustive in identifying the approaches (ignoring a few particularly exotic ones) but will not be so exhaustive in presenting examples; whenever possible, we have chosen systems that we are familiar with.

We will be describing techniques and systems to be used for producing animation for the media of films or television. We will thus not be discussing plotter and static graphics or their enormous amounts of associated software. Systems limited to slide production will similarly be omitted.

GAME PLAN

We will first define and contrast real-time versus stored-time (non-real-time) operation, indicating the trades-off inherent in each approach. Then, in the same manner, vector (line drawing) graphics, raster (TV format) graphics and real-time regeneration (stand alone) graphics will each be analyzed for their applicability. To cross-reference this material, we will isolate and give examples of the following combinations:

Film/Vector
Film/Raster
Video/Vector
Video/Raster

Finally, to summarize the concepts further, we will discuss what is available for your money. To simplify this discussion, we will use the following labels to identify levels of capital expenditure (and, co-incidentally, access):

Personal:	Under $5,000
Small Institutional:	$5,000 to $20,000
Large Institutional:	$20,000 to $200,000
Hollywood/Military:	Over $200,000

As a partial disclaimer, please note that we, in our own thinking are committed to real-time systems. In fact, our own systems have never been sophisticated enough to operate in anything but real-time. Also, for clarity of exposition, we have chosen to generalize extensively in this chapter, painfully aware of how easy it is to contradict generalizations by giving counterexamples. Please feel free to disagree with us at will.

REAL-TIME VERSUS STORED TIME

We define a real-time system as one in which the user has the opportunity to affect the result as it is happening. Feedback is an inherent part of real-time systems.

A stored-time system does not allow the user to affect the outcome as it is happening. Such systems do not have tight feedback loops in the human-machine interface. In other words, the visualization of the image is separated from its creation by a processing time which exceeds, nominally, one-thirtieth of a second. Of course, many tasks with feedback loops of a tenth of a second or more are considered real-time. Stored-time systems in computer graphics have processing times that can range from several minutes to days.

An example of a stored time system is a microfilm plotter. It takes anywhere from several hours to days to see the output, and no changes can be made in the output until it is seen. Broadcast television, even if it is covering live events, is not real-time either, because the viewer (user) has no control over the incoming images. Using a TV camera yourself is real-time, however, as are most of the tasks we do everyday like driving, turning on light switches, washing dishes, drawing, and so on.

Advantages of Real-Time Systems

1. Interaction is possible.

2. Rich feedback systems allow humans to deal with very complex technology without understanding its underlying mechanism. The user can concentrate effort on understanding the implications of his choices rather than the technicalities of how they are accomplished. It is in the nature of human beings to require rich feedback.

3. The learning process is continual and rapid with real-time systems. The user is informed of what to do by how far off his goal he is.

4. Performances are possible.

Disadvantages of Real-Time Systems

1. Real-time systems need enormously detailed human engineering which is often not available, or even not yet properly understood.

2.   Real-time systems sometimes require the human to control more than is possible.

3.   The design constraints of real-time systems in terms of bandwidth and speed of digital computers prohibits the use of techniques that require more than a thirtieth of a second or so to compute.

Advantages of Stored-Time Systems

1. Techniques that take considerable computer time can be utilized. Most computer graphics now take considerable amounts of computer time per frame.

2.   Cost/performance can be adjusted toward the computer side; this is often needed to meet the design requirements of a particular project.

3.   Some people claim that operating in stored-time forces a contemplative attitude towards producing images, because it requires accurate prediction of the results in lieu of experiencing them. One has, of necessity, more time to examine the details. There is an analogy in music: composing versus improvising.

Disadvantages of Stored-Time Systems

1. Considerable skill is required to master the operating system of the computer. This operating system has often been specially modified to cope with computer graphics and these modifications are not always stable. On a time-shared system graphics users are seldom popular.

2.   It takes much longer to produce materials. Every mistake is a delay, and, even without a mistake, a system that requires one minute per frame needs thirty hours to make one minute of finished work at thirty frames per second.

Summary – Real-Time versus Stored-Time

Most practical systems use both real-time and stored-time techniques. Some allow real-time previews in 'wireframe' and produce the shaded half-tone images at their leisure. Others allow real-time input (as in paint programs) but slower recording. Many systems produce short segments in real-time which are later edited together, rather than attempt long continuous streams. The terminology nevertheless is useful in describing systems and their user interface details.

VECTOR DRAWING SYSTEMS

Vector drawing systems, also called line drawing systems, draw pictures by connecting specified line end points. They draw in a conceptual sense much like humans do, point to point, a line at a time.

There are two dominant types of vector displays:

1. Stored image
   a. Direct view storage tubes (e.g. Tektronix)
   b. Plasma Panels (as used by PLATO system).
   c. Scan Conversion Memories (Hughes, Princeton, etc.)

2. Refreshed image
    a. Conventional (e.g. Evans & Sutherland, Vector General, Adage, Imlac, 3 Rivers, many more).
    b. Beam penetration colour systems.
    c. Shadow mask systems (Evans & Sutherland).

Newman & Sproull have detailed descriptions of these technologies — we will concentrate on the production-related aspects.

Storage tubes require time to erase images or parts of images; this limits the scope for animation of images. It is often difficult to erase part of an image without affecting other parts. Direct view storage tubes require the whole screen to be erased, and the other types, while allowing selective erase, do not take account of overlapping lines, so erasure of one line which crosses another line leaves a hole in the remaining line. Storage displays are generally available in the Small Institutional, and, as of late, in the high-end Personal range. They are also commonly available on time-sharing remote systems, or systems running directly off local microprocessors and mini-computers. Storage tubes are now a dying technology and are being replaced by single-colour video systems; the next edition of this book will probably not mention them.

Refreshed Image tubes require the image to be continually redrawn, that is, refreshed. If it is not refreshed within 1/30 second, the decay of the tube of phosphorescence, and the failure of the persistence of vision, causes the display to 'blink' objectionably. Refresh image tubes require, in general, mini-computers dedicated to the display management. Occasionally, small time-sharing systems are used, but the display still has to be within 10 metres of the computer. It is not unusual to have one of these displays hog half the bus time of a dedicated mini-computer.

The Large Institution cost of refresh systems is partially dictated by the need for mini-computer support. Many of these systems come complete with mandatory small mini-computer, since the interfacing is easier if it is standardized. Furthermore, even a small mini-computer is as good at handling the interrupts and the refreshing as a large IBM 370 computer

The chief benefit of refresh displays is that they automatically erase themselves, so that the refreshed image can be different without any additional time or effort on the part of the display. Discounting the time it takes to compute the image (for translations, scaling and even rotation and perspective, these computations are sometimes performed with appropriate hardware) it is as fast to change the image as not. Thus, refresh display systems are capable of doing significant real-time graphics.

Implicit in the choice of a vector drawing system is that line drawings are required. (Ten years ago, when only vector systems were available, this choice was forced). Humans have been using lines to communicate pictorial information longer than they have used written words. The human perceptual system seems to be geared toward edge detection and line extraction, so that the abstraction of images to lines, as one does in newspaper cartoons and engineering drawings, is valid because of the information is efficiently transferred in line drawings. When stored in a computer, only the end points and connection information for these lines need be stored, leading to great economies in memory use.

As an example of the efficiency of vector displays, it takes a sequence of six number pairs to draw a five-pointed star, independent of resolution and size. On a raster system, exactly dependent on resolution, it takes anywhere from four thousand to four million numbers to draw a star. Not to be misleading, though, if you draw with shading or use lots of curves (which have to be broken down into short lines or even points) the vector approach can require enormous numbers of endpoints. For instance, simulating a black and white television image with a vector display requires about 750,000 numbers and cannot be done in real-time by currently available hardware (we are figuring 512 x 512 times three for x, y position and intensity). Raster displays gain efficiency by assuming the x and y position, thus requiring only intensity information to be given.

Given that for your application, drawing lines is optimal, or at least acceptable, the following advantages and disadvantages apply:

Advantages of vector drawing systems

1.   Excellent resolution. Vector drawing systems have resolutions varying from 512 (plasma) to several thousand lines per screen.

2.   Good transformation capability: rotation, scaling, translation, perspective, etc. are simplified because transforming the image requires transforming only the endpoint data. Hardware to do the transformations exists on the high-end systems.

3.   No staircasing of lines. Lines are drawn with analogue techniques (except plasma) so they are smooth and do not exhibit the stepping that is a side-effect of digital line drawing.

4.   Selective erase on refresh displays is a matter for the software.

Disadvantages of vector drawing systems

1.   Realism is difficult to obtain.

2.   The flicker limit on refresh displays restricts the image complexity in real-time drawing.

3.   Refresh display vectors 'pile-up'. This results in intensity variations based on how many vectors cross — this makes adding colour by intensity separation difficult.

4.   The background is always black.

5.   A programming error which leaves the beam stationary can burn a hole in the phosphor, permanently damaging the tube.

VIDEO RASTER SYSTEMS

Raster systems are based on television technology. Conceptually they simulate television cameras in that the computer provides a stream of numbers specifying sequential colour and intensity values which cause a television monitor to scan out an image.

The dominant types of refresh displays are:

1. Frame buffers (Evans & Sutherland, Genisco, DeAnza, Sigma, etc.).
2. Run-length encoded systems (mainly custom built, Three Rivers).
3. Character-generator type (Tektronix, video games).

We will discuss each type in detail.

Frame Buffers

Frame buffers are distinguished by the fact that they have one storage cell in memory for each point (the pixel) on the screen. Thus, there is a fixed reference in memory for each geometrical point. Frame buffer displays always include hardware to scan the memory fast enough to produce a television signal. It is conceptually the simplest raster device, but it requires relatively vast amounts of memory. It takes the same amount of memory to store the simplest and the most complex images. Furthermore, each time the range of choice of intensity or colour value is doubled, so the memory requirement doubles. For 525-line video, this is nominally 250,000 numbers. (Note that the concept of number here becomes sloppy because it is the precision of the number that determines the range of colours and intensities available on the screen at any one time. The terminology of bits and bytes more accurately reflects the memory requirements. We will avoid bits and bytes and talk about different colour levels. You can convert to bits by taking the base two logarithm, if you wish).

The cost of a frame buffer is closely correlated to the amount of memory it uses. Personal systems like the Apple and Bally and some 256 x 256 by 16 colour systems are available for around $1,000 or less. Small institutions can now afford 512 x 512 by 256, (2^8), colour systems which can fully approximate black and white television (by assigning the whole colour range to the grey scale). To exercise the colour capability of a colour monitor, one needs about twice as much memory (giving over 65,000, (2^{16}), colours).

The chief advantage of frame buffers is that the value of each point on the display can be totally uncorrelated with any other point, thus allowing maximum generality of imaging.

Run-length displays

Many images have a high correlation between adjacent pixels. Uniform background colours, large filled in areas, and block letters are common in graphics, particularly when drawing charts and graphs. Hardware can be added to the display which condenses the image into lists of runs of a single colour intensity. This is called 'run-length' encoding. For example,the first twenty lines of a display might be blue background. A run-length display might require just two memory words to describe the approximately 10,000 pixels in the first twenty lines. A frame buffer would still require the 10,000 numbers to be all set in blue. (In fact, most frame buffer systems use run-length encoding to store images on computer tape or discs because of the economy). However, to run-length encode a worst-case image like tight vertical stripes takes at least twice the memory of a frame buffer. Typically, run-length displays are used only when the memory saving is expected to be around 90% over frame buffer technology. The choice of system then hinges on being able to predict the complexity of the image.

Memory costs have been dropping consistently. Run-length systems are losing favour because even small changes to the image requires extensive rebuilding of the run-length list, whereas, with frame buffers, only the relevant pixels need be changed. Furthermore, smooth shading and texturing, which require high pixel-to-pixel nonconformity, are inefficient to run-length encode. One example of a highly refined run-length system is ANIMA II (CSURI77).

Character-generator-type Displays

As is the case with alphanumeric video terminals for computers in which the information is encoded as repetitions of symbols, one can achieve economies of memory by restricting images to combinations of symbols of a certain size. Chess and checker games are an obvious example and, in fact, this technology is used by the very low-end video game resolution with single intensity.

The primary reason for using character-generator-type technology is to increase resolution in sparse, or spatially redundant, applications.

At this time, most media image applications use frame buffers; the software is simpler to implement, in general, and frame buffers lend themselves to texturing and other devices which contribute to realism.

Advantages of Raster Drawing Systems (Frame Buffers in particular)

> 1. Texturing and photographic realism possible

> 2. Can simulate low-resolution vector drawing systems (the reverse is not true).

> 3. Potential compatibility with television for 'scanning in' images, combining and storing of images.

Disadvantages of Raster Drawing Systems

> 1. Massive memory requirements and transmission times: 512 x 512 one-colour display takes 14.5 minutes over 300 baud telephone line, 13.6 seconds over a 19.2K baud high speed terminal interface line.

> Colour images can require up to fifteen million 8-bit numbers per second, that is 150 million baud, for real-time transmission. This represents 900 million 8-bit numbers per minute, and this would occupy all the storage of a very large computer system.

> 2. Large scale changes in the image are time-consuming.

> 3. Geometric transformations on anything but the whole frame at once are difficult and very time-consuming. Certain systems with very sophisticated memory addressing modes can do full frame translations and scaling in real time, and, in theory, even 2-D rotations and perspective of the slit-scan type.

> 4. Diagonal lines and edges of objects exhibit 'staircasing'. Time-consuming software techniques and additional intensity or colour range per point are needed to soften the staircasing effect to the point where it is not objectionable. Staircasing is particularly noticeable in animation graphics because the edges appear to crawl.

Summary — Vector versus Raster Systems

Vector displays were invented for engineering applications and are excellent for displaying high-resolution black and white images of line drawings. One has to spend a million dollars to get the real-time capability in a raster system (at 1024 x 1024 resolution) that is routinely available for $70,000 in high-end vector systems.

Raster systems were invented for more general purposes and thus are more easily adaptable to media production needs of realism. One pays heavily for the realism, however, in computer time and by giving up real-time production, at least until the technology advances.

FILM, VIDEO AND REAL-TIME REGENERATION

In this section we will discuss the relative merits of film and video recording and real-time regeneration (local computer graphics display as a medium). We presume the reader is familiar with film and video recording formats, costs and resolutions. These concepts will be used freely but not explained in detail.

FILM

Some early movies made from computers were composed of still-frames taken off paper plotter output. This method has obvious registration and contrast problems and is very time consuming, since plotters are very slow.

A much simpler technique is to point a movie camera at a vector or raster display screen. Tubes designed for human viewing are usable but not ideal. Film movement must be synchronized with the display to avoid shutter bars. Cathode ray tubes are curved and this geometric distortion is quite easily seen in filmed pictures from these tubes.

These problems can be avoided by using a microfilm plotter, which is, in essence, a small, flat, high-precision tube with a camera calibrated and fixed to it. Often computer-controlled optical filters are used to give colour. Both raster and vector techniques are used in microfilm plotters.

Advantages of film as a recording medium

1. Time integration. Time-exposure photographic techniques allow very complex, slowly-built images to be constructed, even if they never visibly exist as a complete entity. Time-lapse photography allows these frames to be played back much faster, thus permitting a relatively slow computer system (that is, nearly every computer system now in existence) to generate highly complex animated images.

2. Film formats are reasonably internationally standardised.

3. Film is capable of high resolution. 3000 lines or more (not line pairs) is common with 35mm film.

4. Film to TV conversion is easy.

5. Large audience projection is easy.

6. Same techniques make slides.

7. Film is the oldest technology and the best understood.

8. Initial investment at the low-cost end is possible (Super-8).

Disadvantages of film as a recording medium

1. Film is not real-time — processing time is from several hours to several days.

2. Film stock and processing is expensive per minute and getting worse.

3. Strobing (temporal aliasing) is an artifact of film sampling.

4. Emulsions need to be matched to maintain even colour.

5. Laboratory processing too often fails because colour temperature is hard to specify. Film labs too often lose or scratch film.

6. Special effects are very time consuming and inaccessible to most people.

7. Sound is time-consuming to include.

8. Cameras and projectors are mechanical and jam and break.

9. Film is not good for office use or small group viewing.

10. Film is highly evolved and will not be significantly improved by technology, nor will cost go down.

VIDEO

The most obvious way to record computer graphics on video is directly from a compatible raster system. Unfortunately many raster systems choose to utilize non-standard video so one must scan-convert, that is, point a television camera at the display device. Although there is generally no synchronization problem, since the TV camera has a certain amount of lag, curvature of the screen still introduces geometric distortion and one must be very careful to avoid loss of brilliance, colour and sharpness when scan converting. One can also point a TV camera at a vector display although this is primarily useful only when the display is real-time. This technique is also called 'scan-converting', although it is more accurately just scanning.

Advantages of video recording

1. Video is real-time — you can verify results immediately.

2. TV camera tube (vidicon) does anti-staircasing automatically (and does not strobe like film) when scan-converting.

3. Video is the dominant means of information transfer today. Receivers are everywhere. (Of course, one can easily transfer film to video).

4. Tape is cheap and reusable.

5. Special effects are relatively easy and accessible.

6. Sound is easy to include (even stereo!).

7. Daytime roomlight viewing possible.

8. Video is likely to undergo moderate performance/price improvement especially with videodisc as a distribution medium — film to video first).

Disadvantages of video recording

1. Analogue, not digital, recording is the most common technique.

2. Expensive (but not impossible) to do time-lapse. You need a read/write video disc or very fancy recorder, both of which are over $50,000 and either do not work well or are custom items. Electronic Still Stores (Ampex) cost over $250,000 to store 30 seconds of video digitally.

3. Nearly impossible to do time exposures. Display device must be capable of presenting the entire image at once.

4. Poor international standardization.

5. Projection is expensive and relatively rare.

6. Video to film conversion is expensive and difficult.

7. Recorders have severe maintenance problems.

8. Lower resolution than in film (comparable to 16mm).

9. Editing system costs puts video out of personal budget, although one can rent time fairly reasonably.

REAL-TIME REGENERATION

As micro-computer displays get cheaper than film projectors and videotape players, it makes sense to consider them as playback devices in their own right. Instead of recording images frame by frame, these devices are most efficiently used by providing streams of instructions which the computer interprets into text, boxes, lines, circles and so on. Animations are generally done by changing parts of the picture rather than the whole frame and are currently rather primitive except in the case of multi-million dollar flight simulation systems. These simulators do quite realistic imaging in real-time on high-resolution colour displays.

Real-time regeneration systems can be used stand-alone and fed from local mass storage (floppy disks, audio cassette tape, etc.) or connected to larger computers over telephone lines.

Advantages of Real-Time Regeneration systems

1. Significant interaction with user is possible, as in viewdata, computer-assisted instruction systems, flight simulators and video games.

2. No 'dub loss' in copying, unlike analogue recording systems.

3. Potentially little or no maintenance except on local mass storage device, if any.

4. Capable of being used in performance context.

5. Likely to undergo dramatic improvements in performance/price ratio.

Disadvantages of Real-Time Regeneration systems

1. No time integration or editing possible – can use techniques suitable for real-time graphics.

2. With the exception of recent ACM/SIGGRAPH standardization efforts aimed at sophisticated systems, no standardization of software exists so one must own the type of terminal for which the software was written.

3. Connections to other systems slow and expensive.

Summary — Film versus Video

For all practical purposes, for most people, film is used for stored-time and video is used for real-time recording. The other advantages and disadvantages are relatively minor in comparison.

CROSS-REFERENCING THE TECHNOLOGIES OF RECORDING AND GRAPHICS

This section is meant to cross-reference the previously enumerated advantages and disadvantages of film/video and raster/vector by indicating synergistic advantages and disadvantages of the four combinations:

Film/Vector	Film/Raster
Video/Vector	Video/Raster

Examples of systems using these combinations will illustrate the trades-off. The section will further cross-reference this material by identifying capabilities affordable by Personal, Small Institutional, and Hollywood/Military budgets.

No attempt is made to make the examples exhaustive. We have simply chosen examples we know well.

FILM/VECTOR

Advantages of filming vector displays

1. Oldest and best-known technology.

2. Best resolution available.

3. Well-suited to stored time. Can use small computer with little memory to generate complex images.

Disadvantages of filming vector displays

1. Filming in real-time is difficult to synchronize.

2. Vector displays designed for human viewing often do not have enough red to produce good colour by filtration. Colour by optical printing is difficult and has registration problems, especially noticeable in the case of bright lines on a black background.

3. Backgrounds are almost always black. Any other colouring requires complex matting and/or optical printing.

4. Considerable attention must be paid to exposure, especially when filming off a display designed for human viewing. Light meters do not work well on vector displays.

5. Care must be taken to ensure that all the detail visible on the display is ultimately viewable in the presentation context, in this case, film projection.

Example 1

Super-8 shot off a Tektronix 4010 ($5,000) terminal hooked to a PDP-11 Unix time-sharing system: Dr. Lou Katz of Columbia University (New York) has produced a number of films meant for presentation at conferences in conjunction with papers concerning molecular interaction. The films are shot in colour but without filtration so that the only colour is green on black. The camera used is a $225 Eumig 830XL (now available as a Bolex) which automatically time-exposes (five seconds in this case) whenever a pulse is sent to trip the camera. A custom-built interface (cost: $100) to the bell on this terminal provided the pulse. Given a build-up time of thirty seconds per frame for a molecule of several hundred vectors over a 1200 baud line, 35 seconds per frame was common. The film was then transferred to videotape using a Kodak VPX. Lou used the C language for this work. This style of production is appropriate to small institutional budgets.

Example 2

A similar method was used by the Senses Bureau, a student group at the University of California at San Diego under the direction of Kent Wilson, to produce a 16mm film about pollution of the Los Angeles basin. The film was shot with a Bolex 16mm camera and colour was added in a film laboratory. There was no pin registration so the different colours visibly jittered around a bit. The computer was an IBM 1800 and the software was FORTRAN. This is a production capability easily affordable by a small institution.

Example 3

16mm filming of a Vector General display, Guenther Tetz at the University of Illinois at Chicago Circle uses a recycled 16mm double-pin registered instrumentation camera (used cost: $1000) interfaced to the PDP-11 mini-computer via an external drive shaft driven by a clutch motor (Hurst PCDA60, cost: $30). The computer tells the motor to advance and senses the position by reading two optical sensors sitting over holes in the disks which indicate shutter open and shutter closed positions. The interface electronics were built by undergraduate students. The software is GRASS.

Example 4

Larry Cuba used a 35mm Mitchell animation camera to film the Briefing Room sequence of zooming down the Death Star trench in perspective for the movie **Star Wars**. The procedure was similar to example 3, using the same hardware and software, except that a wire attached to a lighted function-switch was used to trigger the animation motor. Larry also used an inexpensive time-lapse video recorder intended for security applications to verify the progress of the animation. This was clearly a Hollywood-style effort.

Example 5

The Dicomed D48 and Information International FR80 microfilm plotters offer high-resolution (up to 4000 lines), high-quality cameras and good optical filtration for colour under computer control, all in an integrated package. Several film formats may be used. These are expensive ($100,000) devices which are quite capable of keeping super-computers busy. For media-production purposes,

Lawrence Livermore Laboratory and New York Institute of Technology use the Dicomed, and Los Alamos Scientific Laboratory and Information International themselves use the FR80. These devices also do raster/film, and are found in mostly Hollywood/Military installations.

Summary

Film/Vector is particularly suited to high-complexity line drawings (circuit board design, drafting, stick-figure molecules, etc.) It is the only combination with enough software commonly available to enable someone who does not want to hire a graphics programmer, or become one, to do computer graphics media production. The emergence of raster graphics, especially with personal systems, will no doubt tip the scales towards raster displays for media production.

FILM/RASTER

Film/raster has recently become popular due to the increase in activity in raster graphics and the decrease in memory costs.

Advantages of filming raster displays

1. Time-lapse capability works well with the typically slow raster graphics systems.

2. Using time-exposure, one can get more colours by changing the colour map while the shutter is open, thus making sophisticated anti-staircasing possible with less memory per pixel.

3. Film can record 1000 x 1000 raster images that video normally cannot.

4. Colour is handled well, colour backgrounds and filled-in areas are easy.

Disadvantages of filming raster displays

1. Synchronization of film to raster needs careful detailing.

2. Colour compensation tables are needed to get the colour on film that you see on the raster display device in video.

Example 1

Super-8 camera filming a Bally Arcade video game programmed in the BASIC language. The $350 Bally Arcade (160 x 102 by four colours) can trigger a Eumig 830XL by sending an audio tone from the earphone plug on the TV to a relay which closes a switch to advance the shutter. To avoid a shutter bar, a time-exposure of a half-second is used, necessitating neutral density filtering or dimming of the TV considerably, since the aperture on this, and other Super-8 cameras of like capability will not close down in the time-exposure mode. This sytem for making computer graphics comes to less than $1000, including a colour TV.

Example 2

16mm camera filming an eight-colour TV display. Ken Knowlton at Bell Laboratories in New Jersey has produced several films using a 16mm Acme animation camera controlled by the display. The display triggers the film to advance, turns off the TV image, waits for the shutter to signal 'open' and then turns the image on for a set number of frames (usually 9-11). The TV is then blanked off and the shutter is once again closed and the film advanced. The turning off and on of the image eliminates the 'shutter-bar' problems seen with free-running cameras. The exposure usually takes 1.5 sec/frame including shutter movement and Ken estimates 2-17 sec/frame for image build-up.

Example 3

The FR80 and Dicomed D48 film recorders previously discussed do high-resolution colour raster graphics as well. Exquisite work has lately come from the Jet Propulsion Laboratory, New York Institute of Technology, Information International Inc., and Livermore Laboratory, complete with highlighting, surface texturing, shading, reflections, transparency, anti-staircasing, and even 'neonizing', lightning bolts and other types of flash. These sytems are Hollywood/Military in budget and the software is largely FORTRAN or C, developed at great expense.

Summary

Film/Raster spans the greatest range of cost/image-complexity, a position it is likely to maintain until the time-lapse recording of video is greatly simplified and/or higher resolution video systems become routinely available. Thus, except for the escalating cost of film and its non-real-time nature, Film/Raster is the currently preferred technology for the high-end and low-end media production.

VIDEO/VECTOR

Video/Vector is the least common of the four possibilities we discuss. Computer scientists are not particularly at home with video in general, and this type of recording situation requires video expertise to do the scan conversion acceptably.

Advantages of video recording a vector display

1. Given a real-time vector system, the process is more or less like videotaping anything — very rich feedback.

2. Superimposition with other images is easy.

3. Can incorporate general video tricks with vector graphics.

Disadvantages of video recording a vector display

1. Non-real time graphics require single-frame videotaping which needs at least a custom tape recorder or Electronic Still Store.

2. Limited to TV resolution.

3. Real-time working means very sophisticated software/hardware configuration or very

simple graphics.

Example 1

Scan Conversion Memory with a video-out port for recording an image building up. Lou Katz and Bill Etra have successfully recorded computer graphics from a Tektronix Scan conversion Memory (conceptually a Tektronix display physically coupled to a video pickup tube inside a light-proof box) attached to a Tektronix 4010 controlled from Unix. Animation is not possible in real-time, but interesting images can be built. These devices are in the Small Institutional range in this configuration.

Example 2

TV camera pointing at a Vector General display. We have developed a short-order media production facility centered around a Vector General PDP-11/45 using the GRASS language. We point one or more TV cameras at the Vector General and mix the outputs with the Sandin Image Processor, which adds colour and does various special effects. This system has produced many hours of material for educational and artistic purposes. The Vector General is a Large Institutional budget device although the Image Processor is in the Personal to Small Institutional range. The major advantage of this approach is the speed at which relatively sophisticated scientific animation can be produced. Furthermore, the real-time aspects make those aesthetic judgements feasible that are difficult to make when using a stored time system.

Summary

The fact that the major example of Video/Vector is a system that is basically the only one of its kind indicates that it meets the requirements of a very specialised environment. This techno-logy is suitable for producing lots of low-cost scientific animation and certain types of non-representa-tional special effects.

VIDEO/RASTER

With the advent of television-compatible display devices, the connection to video recor-ders and broadcast or closed circuit TV is inevitable.

Advantages of video recording raster scan displays

1. The graphics are directly recordable (no cameras!) if the display puts out the right video format.

2. Usable in real-time situations.

Disadvantages of video recording raster scan displays

1. Time-lapse difficult, as previously indicated.

Of course, these are in addition to all the advantages/disadvantages of video and raster graphics by them-selves.

Example 1

Recording directly off a Bally Arcade connected through the antenna connector on the tape deck. This approach gives reasonable quality video with quasi-static displays. Such a system costs about $1000 if you already have a TV.

Example 2

Time-lapse video recording of photo-realism quality animation at New York Institute of Technology. Using a custom IVC9000 2" Helical scan tape recorder under computer control, wonderfully complex images input by skilled cel animators can be recorded. 512 x 512 frame buffers with 256 shades of each of red, green and blue are painted into by artists using electronic tablets with very sophisticated software. This is a large institutional to Hollywood/Military configuration, and is described in Chapters 4 and 5.

Non-example

As a non-example, many raster systems do not bother to conform to any TV standard and thus are difficult or impossible to record. The Apple II personal computer, for example, not only encodes colour peculiarly, it also puts out the wrong number of lines. TV receivers are much more tolerant than tape recorders. Beware!

CAPABILITY/BUDGET CONSIDERATIONS

Most people actually come to computer graphics with a certain amount of money to spend. This section is meant further to cross-reference the data and help you decide if you are spending too much or too little for the capability you want.

Personal Systems (Under $5,000)

1. Stored-time film/vector on time-sharing system, Super 8 or 16mm camera. This is a good choice if timesharing is available easily, monochrome visuals are acceptable, time is no object and graphical quality is negotiable.

2. Video/Raster or Film/Raster or low resolution. This system works well if low resolution, limited animation and computationally simple colour graphics using local processing are acceptable.

Small Institutional Systems ($5,000 – $20,000)

1. Film/Vector systems in this range have small mini-computers with simple vector refresh displays.

2. Video/Vector systems using scan conversion memories fall into this budget category.

3. Raster systems with film or video get to 256 x 256 by 16 colours complete with mini- or micro-processor, floppy disks and decent amount of memory (64,000 words).

By going up to $20,000, the severe limitations of personal systems are softened. Higher resolution, more (but still primitive) animation capability, and increased local processing power become available.

Large Institutional Systems ($20,000 − $200,000)

    1. Film/Vector now has good quality refresh tubes and high-resolution microfilm recorders.

    2. Video/Vector systems are practical real-time animation systems with specialized use.

    3. Raster systems for film and video recording go up to 512 x 512 or 640 x 480 resolution with 256 to 16 million colours, with no improvement in real-time capability because increased resolution absorbs all increases in computer speed that higher-priced computers provide. Microfilm recorders and time-lapse video available at the high-end.

Hollywood/Military Systems ($200,000 − $2,000,000 per system).

    1. Low-end gets you customized systems for production, rather than experimental purposes.

    2. High-end has real-time high-resolution full-colour 3-D simulation systems suitable for flight trainers and, eventually, for fantasy creation (war).

SOFTWARE

    It may be noticeable by now that little attention has been given to the computer software costs. Unless the software you want comes with the system (very rare) the time and effort expended on software development will far exceed both the time spent procuring the hardware and the money spent buying it. Computer graphics systems are simply unusable without full software support, except for demos, of course.

    Computer graphics systems usually use FORTRAN with graphic extensions. One must learn programming to a level of fluency which allows one to subvert the language's general inapplicability to the task of graphics. Of all the computer graphic languages developed, none are generally available and few exist at more than three computer installations. Those that might be sprung loose are usually carefully tailored to their hardware, graphics being such a test of machines and programming.

    All this is not surprising since there is not a single manufacturer whose cash flow is dependent on animation graphics. Nor is there currently a market for animation languages. The understandable lack of standardization in this dynamic field defeats the exportability of software. One has to copy a system in all its details to use the software on it.

    Aside from proprietary software which one cannot buy, there is free software in the public domain generated by government-supported research. Too often, however, free software has insufficient documentation and nobody to ask how to make the inevitable minor modifications, much less fix the bugs.

    The conclusion is that one has to either buy equipment and write extensive software, or rent equipment, software, and technicians by the hour from one of the small but growing number of computer animation speciality houses. Whether this situation is temporary is a matter for conjecture.

EPILOGUE

Despite the software swamp, the increasing availability of exciting computer graphics hardware is encouraging. Software development, for many people, is very rewarding and beats chess and glass bead games hands down. Decreasing hardware costs means access will improve geometrically and the consumerization of computers will mean that most of the hardware and software problems we currently face will soon have been solved. The technical capabilities of flight simulators will filter down as very large-scale integrated circuits become common. It is not too early to start learning about computer graphics.

The following illustrations, reproduced in black and white from colour originals, exemplify some of the systems mentioned in this chapter.

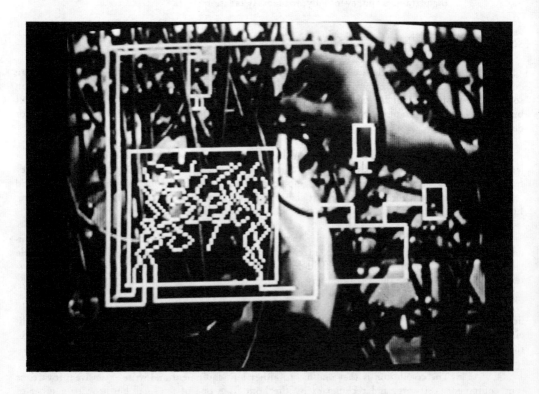

Example of low-end personal raster graphics combined with real live television. This image was taken from a videotape playback. Note the staircasing of diagonal lines on the graphics but not, of course, on the analogue TV image. Artist : Jane Veeder.   Video/Raster

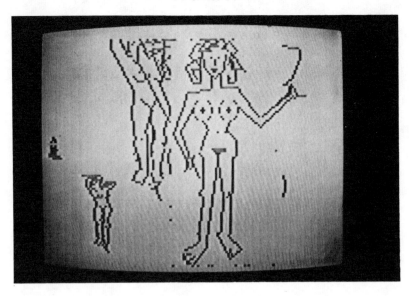

Example of a line-drawn image interactively constructed in real time with a simple joystick drawing program. This photo also shows raster simulation of low-resolution (160 x 102) vector drawing, with obvious staircasing of diagonal lines. It was done on a Bally Zgrass unit in the personal budget range and is part of a three-minute animation recorded directly on videotape. Artist : Copper Gilroth.

Video/Raster

The same system and artist as the photograph above. A good candidate for run length encoding and a difficult (although not impossible) image to do on a vector system. Note the staircasing on the antenna, and the background which is not black.

A vector image displayed on the Vector General 3DR system showing high resolution on a mandatory black background, intensity change from vector pileup and non-staircased diagonals. This system is available in the large institutional budget range.   Artist : Guenther Tetz.   **Film/Vector**

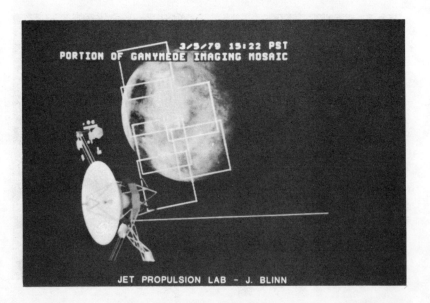

This higher-resolution raster image shows anti-staircased lines (note details on space craft) and was done by time-integration on film, with a large institutional budget.   **Film/Raster**

Example of output from a flight simulator using raster graphics with texturing and realism. This image was done on a military budget.   **Real time/Raster**

Example of mixing a video image of a dancer with vector graphics rotating and recording in real time. It is from a performance by five people. Analogue oscillator patterns are video mixed into the dancer's body. Artists : Tom DeFanti, Dan Sandin, Jane Veeder, Phil Morton and Rylin Harris.   **Video/Vector**

COMPUTER CHARACTER ANIMATION -- IS IT POSSIBLE ?

Edwin Catmull

Lucasfilm

For more than 10 years, attempts have been made to computerise the traditional animation process. There have been many notable advances in this time, including the solving of the hidden surface problem and the development of the frame buffer, but the original objectives for computer animation have not yet been met. In this chapter, some of the reasons for this are examined.

Animation has become an established and recognised tool for film makers. It works on a lot of levels and is now almost part of our cultural heritage. From the Saturday morning TV cartoons, through education and instruction, to the perfection of **Fantasia** or **Pinocchio**, there is a continuity of technique that gives these images their particular style.

There are two ideas that underly this technique. The first is that since the cine camera turns the continuous world into a succession of still pictures, it might be possible to invent a world by just drawing a lot of pictures, photographing them one after the other, and projecting them like an 'ordinary' film. To make something happen in this invented world the pictures must change.

The second idea is that not all changes in a picture are important; only those changes that carry the idea embodied in the images are indispensable. The style of animated, or cartoon, films comes from deciding just what these indispensable movements are and how they can be portrayed with a minimum of labour in the drawing of the pictures. In a feature-length animated film there could be 170,000 frames to be projected. In an exciting (and commercially successful) film something is happening for most of the time so it·is easily possible that 150,000 different frames must somehow be produced. If each frame must be drawn, coloured and photographed by hand in its correct place in the sequence, this can become a monumentally labour-intensive activity and, as such, a natural target for take-over by computer. To understand why 15 years of effort in this direction has been only partially successful it is necessary to examine the traditional process of animation in a little detail.

The animation of Disney, Hanna Barbera and their imitators is all '2-D'. That is to say, every frame is a flat picture in which any depth information is purely artistic. Since the pictures show characters in settings, it is always possible to divide the picture into 'foreground' and 'background'. These are not quite the pictorial descriptions from artistic analysis meaning 'front' and 'rear'; they divide the

61

picture into a fixed background over which the characters are animated. Nothing in the background moves relative to its surroundings. It can get larger or smaller, move to the left, right or any which way, but always as a whole. The rest of the picture contains all those components that move relative to each other and to the background.

The central idea of animation by hand, then, is to compose a picture from a background overlayed by transparent 'cels' on which are painted the components of the moving parts of the image. The great skill is to decompose the moving objects into the smallest number of separate cells such that by making small changes in some of these overlays and using them successively, an adequate impression of the desired motion is conveyed when the frames are projected one after the other at 24 frames per second.

Over the years, a system has evolved that deploys creative and manual talents to their best advantage and also keeps track of the vast number of individual cels and backgrounds (there being as many as 5 separate overlays at once on a background) that are required to tell a story. A central concept in this deployment is inbetweening. The idea is that a movement, such as walking, can be broken down into a (small) number of 'key frames' which characterise the essence of the particular movement and that these can be linked by rather simple interpolations to make a sufficient number of frames to give the desired smoothness and finesse to the movement. Thus there are two types of artistic and creative activity; drawing the key frames and drawing the inbetween frames. Since quite exceptional skill is required to get a sequence right first time, it is common to have a number of check stages, or 'line tests', to ensure that no time is spent painting and filming unsatisfactory sequences.

There is another crucial concept in conventional animation. This is that the pictures are designed to fit the soundtrack. It is economic sense to draw no more pictures than are absolutely necessary and this can be ensured by exactly fixing the soundtrack. Once this has been done, it is possible to specify, to the nearest frame, the mouth movements necessary to give the impression of 'lip-sync', where the words appear to be spoken by the character on the screen. The whole process is, then, a roughly sequential pipeline, with the generation of the backgrounds going on in parallel, composed of the following steps:

1. Story written
2. Storyboard laid out
3. Soundtrack recorded
4. Detailed layout
5. Soundtrack analysed and itemised
6. Key frames specified (Animator)
7. Inbetweens selected and specified (Assistant Animator)
8. Movements completed (Inbetweeners)
9. Line test
10. Outlines transferred to cel
11. Cels painted
12. Check for matches and errors
13. Film sequences
14. Edit sequences to soundtrack.

A movie is made up of sequences and a sequence is made up of scenes. A scene corresponds roughly to 5-30 seconds of uninterrupted action. All of the scenes that belong to the same part of the story make up a sequence.

There are two kinds of paper forms used to control the flow of drawings through the pipeline:

1. The route sheet

Every scene is listed with its length, vital statistics, and the name of the person in charge of the various states. This allows the director quickly to determine the status and location of a scene.

2. The exposure sheet

The exposure sheet has a line on it for every frame in the film. Each line indicates the dialogue for that frame, the order of all figures, the background, and camera position. The exposure sheets are grouped according to scenes.

Some of the procedures used in the process are arbitrary but most are grounded in necessity. For example, an arbitrary procedure is that film is measured in feet rather than seconds or frames. On the other hand, the exposure sheets and routing sheets are needed to control the large amounts of information that must be passed around.

At first sight, this traditional scheme seems to offer several good targets for computerisation. If the pictures could be computerised, then the use of cels to make the overlays could be eliminated, so removing a practical limitation to the complexity of possible animation.

The difficulty is that the computer, at present, has to separate hand and eye. There are now several ways to get data into the computer but the two most important are by way of the touch-tablet and by the direct scanning-in of an image by a TV camera, via analogue-to-digital (ADC) converters, to the computer memory. Artists, however, must be able to paint. Their training has a long history, its own practice and a proven vocabulary. These features must be reproduced in a computerised version. Several workers have devised Painting Programs that try to emulate the artist's pallette. They all involve the use of a stylus on a tablet to produce an image on a TV screen. After years of training, looking at his hand to check and modify the image produced, would the artist readily accept a computer workstation? The answer has been most encouraging: if the station is well designed, if the facilities offered are good and if the results are reliable and reproducible, the answer in practice has been a resounding yes.

Another stage in the traditional animation sequence that might be helped by computerisation appeared to be the colouring of the outline cels. In a computer-generated image, colour information could be an integral part of both the data base and the display device. The problems of colour quality control in the traditional animation studio are severe and the reproducibility offered in principle by digital specification appeared to be a big bonus. It is only since the late 70's that colour display devices have been available to generate images of sufficient resolution to be used on 35mm film stock; however, the possibility of the direct generation of videotape without the intervening film stage, with the Saturday Morning market in mind, opened up entirely new and exciting prospects. In short, at the beginning of the 60's, computer animation looked a real and exciting possibility.

It is safe to say that the hopes raised for the computer storage and display of full colour, full tone images have been realised. The solid-state memory in which each word represents a picture point, the frame buffer, has made possible the easy storage and retrieval of digital data in a variety of forms. The almost universal adoption of raster scan techniques for the output of these memories to film or videotape has made possible the generation of very high quality, full colour images.

The computer generation of the images themselves has not been quite so successful. Two distinct problem areas have emerged. The man-machine interface and the logic of inbetweening. The second problem has already been touched on and will be returned to later. The man-machine interface is not a trivial problem. If a computer system is to be useful, it must be useful to artists. Creative people must be able to work creatively and produce work that has an individual style. A lot of effort has gone into this problem and in at least one institution (New York Institute of Technology) a successful system

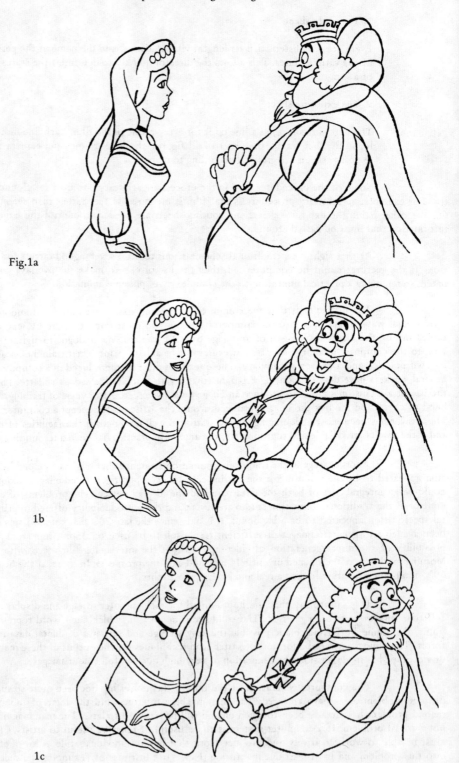

Fig.1a

1b

1c

has been produced.

The most inviting target has always been the inbetweening stage.

The problem seems simple enough: given figures A and C, find the correspondence between the figures such that we can produce an interpolated figure B dependent on the correspondence. This problem might be likened to another well known problem: given Russian and English, find the correspondence between them such that we can transform a sentence from one language to the other. On the face of it the problem seem quite simple but we know that it isn't. Similarly there are subtle problems with inbetweening which require intelligence to resolve.

To illustrate, an animator drew figures 1a and 1c as extremes. The two drawings were given to an assistant animator who produced figure 1b. The drawings would next be given to an inbetweener who would produce three drawings between 1a and 1b and three between 1b and 1c. This example was taken from a real animation situation and is not unusual. A close examination of the drawings will show that automatic inbetweening of full animation is a formidable task.

The principal difficulty is that the animator's drawings are really two-dimensional projections of the three-dimensional characters as visualized by the animator, hence information is lost in each drawing. For example, one leg obscures another. It is the loss of information which severely limits automatic inbetweening. A person can infer the original object from the drawing because he knows what the original model is, i.e. he understands what a leg is. In order for a program to 'understand' a drawing it must contain a model of a character that corresponds to the model in the animator's head. While such a program is not inconceivable it is akin to difficult artificial intelligence problems.

Computer programming has offered intriguing flexibility. Take the concept of 'brush'. Early painting programmes gave the artist a range of 'brushes' such that if the tip of the stylus was moved over the tablet, marks of different thickness, tone, hue and texture could be made, just like the brush on canvas. But the concept of 'brush' can be extended by programming. A leaf can be drawn in some detail defined as a 'brush' and dabbed down over a tree, each dab a leaf. Entry to a separate part of the pallette allows the 'leaves' to be nudged into artistic orientations and then by further simple programming steps 'autumn', for that tree at least, can be programmed, colour changes and all. Painting is now a powerful and proven device in computer animation.

The condition of 'inbetweening' is not so satisfactory. There have been several approaches to the problem.

1. Try to infer the missing information from the line drawings.
2. Require the animators or program operators to specify the missing information by editing.
3. Break the characters into overlays.
4. Use skeletal drawings.
5. Use 3-D outlines and centrelines.
6. Restrict the class of animation that may be drawn.

Each approach needs comment:

1. Infer information

This has already received comment. It should be further noted that human inbetweeners also make mistakes.

2. Editing

The operator must specify the correspondence of the lines and the hidden lines. One must also ensure that during the process of interpolation, the hidden lines become visible in a correct manner. The process is further complicated by extremes where there is no correspondence at all! (See Fig. 1). In this case more extremes are required. Animators trained in the use of the system will know where to put extremes but the overall gain is reduced both because more extremes are required and because an editor must spend time on each drawing.

3. Break character into overlays

This means that the arms, legs, and body may be on separate levels. Someone (probably not the animator) must do the separation. Although this approach takes care of several kinds of problem (i.e. the arms and legs in a walk cycle) it doesn't solve the problem of the rotating head.

4. Skeletons

Several people have suggested skeletons as an approach for easing both input and inbetweening (Ref. 1, 2). The key idea is that a correspondence is established between a fully drawn character and a skeletal outline. It is then only necessary to animate the skeleton. This method handles limited body movement but is not really adequate for changes in feature, expression, the manipulation of non-rigid figures or cloth, or motion involving hidden surfaces and three-dimensional rotation. These capabilities are important, however, for good character animation.

5. 3-D outlines and centrelines

It may be possible to extend the skeleton idea. For a large number of views of a figure a corresponding outline with centreline could be drawn. This would then define a pseudo-three-dimensional character. The animator would draw the outline and centreline following certain rules. The program would determine the appropriate outline from the character definition and hence the character. This is strictly a research topic at present.

6. Restrict the animation

Just avoid troublesome figures or poses. Of course simple figures are also easier to produce conventionally so we may lose a substantial portion of the gain.

In practice, most systems (with one exception) require that the operator specify the correspondence between the lines of two extremes. If there is not a one-to-one correspondence then a new extreme is required. The one exception is that of Stern (Ref. 3) whose system automatically determines correspondence from scanned-in images. In all cases, the problems of incorrect matchup and manual intervention remain.

ANALYSING PROPOSED SOLUTIONS

There are many variations on the above methods. What may seem like a good approach frequently requires some preparation or fixup. In order to evaluate any approach we must introduce the concept of 'touch-time'.

Touch-time is the amount of time that some operator or artist must spend working on a figure in some process. The total touch-time would then be the total of the times spent on all steps of the pipeline. An analysis then requires that we find the average total touch-time per frame. If the computer can perform inbetweening then the average total touch-time goes down. If any method requires some touchup, we must include the touch-up time. The processes included are tracing or figure entry, scanning, colouring or painting, error correction and so on.

Solutions to the various problems of computer-assisted character animation should include analyses of the ramifications of that solution. The full extent of any ramification cannot be fully understood until the method is tried in the environment for which it is intended. Extrapolation of preliminary results will probably yield incorrect conclusions.

The throughput of the animation pipeline is dependent on touch-time per frame, machine time per frame, the number of stations for artists and operators, and the amount of equipment for processing the images. It is not a simple matter just to state that the computer makes animation cheaper and faster. Cost-effective computer-assisted character animation has yet to be demonstrated.

Another part of any analysis should be a statement regarding the class of characters to be handled. The ease with which any algorithm can be used is dependent on the complexity of characters and the quality of movement. It is necessary to understand any restrictions on characters before one can evaluate the approach used to animate them.

My contribution to the problem has been to try and devise a system that embodies the basic structure of the classical animation processes whilst giving the artist control over the automatic generation of the inbetweened images at every stage. Called TWEEN, the system is a key-frame animation system in which the artist draws or enters key-frames and the computer interpolates to provide missing drawings. The database management, exposure sheet, and route sheet are an integral part of the system. It was developed in conjunction with professional animators.

Once a specified number of inbetweens has been produced, the artists reviews them in sequence on the graphic display processor. If an inbetween is wrong, the artist makes the necessary modifications with the electronic pen and considers the corrected drawing an extreme. The computer is then told to redraw the remaining inbetweens to the next extreme so that they too will be corrected.

The artist can immediately check the animation of extremes and inbetweens by specifying an electronic pencil test at the animation station. The screen of the graphics display processor presents all the drawings in rapid sequence for study by the artist. Again, any necessary changes are made in individual drawings until the artist is satisfied with the entire animated scene.

The character artist's task is simplified too because TWEEN permits any number of levels of animation. That is, as in conventional animation, a separate drawing can be provided for each character in a scene or for parts of characters (such as head or legs) in order to simplify the generation of inbetweens that will satisfactorily simulate motion at projection speed.

Conventional animation is limited to five levels of character images because the acetate overlays are not totally transparent. As many as 20 levels have been used in early computer production. (There is no degradation of the image in computer-assisted animation whatever the number of levels).

The exposure sheet used in conventional animation, which includes a row for each frame and a column for each level of animation, specifies the dialogue for that frame and the order of all character images, background and camera position. The exposure sheet for TWEEN is very similar to conventional exposure sheets, including instructions on zooms and pans. The exposure sheets are entered into the system in order to guide the computer in frame-by-frame assembly of the scenes in an animation sequence.

TWEEN is currently being used by an animation team. On average the tween system generates four or five drawings for each one drawn by the artists.

The images TWEEN produces still have to be painted in some way. They are outline drawings that enclose regions to be coloured or textured.

The form of a figure need not only be specified by an outline. This is essentially a calligraphic concept that has been carried over into the computerised image. The coming of the frame buffer has encouraged a new line of development – the representation of objects as convex polyhedra. This method for dividing any real, 3-dimensional, object up into the smallest number of flat planes, each of 3, 4, 5 or 6 sides, has lead to a whole new style of image representation. Great strides have been made in the mathematical analysis of such figures and the restriction to flat patches has been relaxed to allow for continuously curving regions that are characterised by reasonably simple polynomials. Now objects can truly be modelled in three dimensions and the 2-dimensional plane picture required for the film computed from any viewpoint.

These 3-D models contain enough data to solve, in principle, the major conceptual difficulty in the 2-D inbetweening problem – what comes into, and what goes out of, view as the characters 'move' over the background. They also contain enough information to allow the computation of shadows, surface texture and highlights.

A great deal has been published on visible-polygon algorithms. While substantial improvements in these algorithms will continue to be made, the problem is essentially understood. Researchers are finding that the bulk of the computer time is not being spent in hidden-surface calculation, but rather it is being spent on lighting calculations. In order to determine the intensity at any pixel, one must use a relationship between the surface normal, the eye position, and the positions of the light sources. This results in a substantial number of calculations at every pixel on the screen.

These calculations are all, of necessity, based on quite severe approximations. Stupendous amounts of computer time can be expended on lighting and surface calculations and a balance must be struck between computational feasibility and the visual acceptability of the resulting image. For the most part, decomposing the picture into an ordered array of discrete pixels has provivded great economies of description and computation. It has had one deleterious effect – the 'jaggies'.

No discussion of computer animation would be complete without mentioning aliasing, one of the most pervasive problems of computer graphics. The symptoms of aliasing are jagged edges, moire patterns, small objects that pop on and off the screen in time, and 'beaded' lines. There are published methods for reducing these symptoms but new software systems almost always ignore the problem. It is very important to understand that anyone who ignores this problem will regret it.

Again there are trades-off to be made; more pixels per line reduce the jaggedness of lines but increase severely the computation time; spatial resolution can be exchanged for brightness information to give thicker, but smoother lines; the image can be degraded artificially by adding 'noise' to produce acceptable projected images. This last trick highlights a crucial element in film-making that is sometimes forgotten. The eye is not a perfect device. It, in its system with the brain, has strengths and weaknesses that can be exploited with advantage. The works of Richard Gregory and John Frisby are a must for serious imagemakers.

It is now possible to talk of the computer animation studio as a reality. It must have a high speed, medium sized digital computer with access to a lot of disc file space (1 full colour TV image can occupy approximately ½MBy), a large suite of programmes that support work stations, perform 2-D and 3-D calculations on image structures, enhance, encode and compress image data for storage and display, and finally to control the output devices such as film or videotape recorders to accumulate the pictures into a sequence one frame at a time in the right order.

At the present time the demands of the commercial film industry are for Science Fiction of the **Star Wars** kind. The moment is ripe to try and combine all the techniques learnt so far, such as texturing, highlighting, the simulation of shadows and reflections and the animation of motion in order to produce images of very high artistic quality. It is, after all, not too hard to make a realistic image of a Space Invader that no one has ever seen!

REFERENCES

1. N. Burtnyk and M. Wein, Interactive skeleton techniques for enhancing motion dynamics in key frame animation, **CACM** (October 1976).

2. A. Kitching, Computer animation — some new ANTICS, **British Kinematograph Sound and Television Journal, 55** (12), 372-386 (December 1973).

3. Garland Stern, **GAS - A system for computer-aided Keyframe animation**, Ph.D. dissertation, University of Utah (1978).

FACILITIES FOR COMPUTER IMAGEMAKING

This chapter contains reports of three typical facilities houses. They will undertake a wide range of work but each has its own special field of excellence. Some other companies working in this area are indicated.

There is a growing number of companies offering facilities for computer imagemaking. The services range from video frame buffer technology up to the very high quality 35mm film or slide production systems. In addition to the three companies who report in this chapter on their work, there are many others who offer similar facilities or similar equipment. There are also a number of companies who will write programs or implement packages on the customer's machine. A short list can be found in Appendix D.

Computer imagemaking facilities are sometimes available in Universities, Polytechnics and Colleges. For work supported by Science Research Council grants there is an FR80 microfilm plotter available at the Rutherford Laboratory. The University of London Computer Centre has a Calcomp 1670 microfilm plotter that can be used by 'outside' users with prior approval.

High quality slide-making and other business and promotional artwork is undertaken by Information International Inc. The MAGI corporation offer similar facilities and both companies are equipped to make movies.

Some of the best facilities exist at Government Military establishments are are therefore not readily available. Very good work is done by the Lawrence Livermore Laboratories and some details can be obtained on what is available there from Dr Steve Levine.

As DeFanti and Sandin have indicated in Chapter 3, there is almost certainly some way that you can afford to make the images you need.

NEW YORK INSTITUTE OF TECHNOLOGY

NYIT
Computer Graphics Laboratory
P. O. Box 170
Wheatley Road
Old Westbury
New York 11568
USA

Telephone: (516) 686-7644

Contact: Louis Schure
        Administrative Director

Contents:

1. Introduction

The New York Institute of Technology has created a facility for producing animated films and videotapes using computers, special computer graphics equipment, a post-production video studio and a team of artists, researchers and technicians. The facility and its research and production activities are described. There are two parts to the facility: the Computer Graphics Lab and the Video Center, which is a full post-production video studio.

The goal of the Computer Graphics Lab is to assemble hardware and software systems capable of producing cost-effective educational and commercial films of high quality with the unusual visual effects made possible using digital techniques. Recently NYIT produced a half-hour educational film, **Measure for Measure**, which successfully mixed conventional animation with computer-assisted animation using two different methods. In addition, in the last few months several test commercials have been made and aired.

2. The Video Center

The Video Center is a fully-operational studio with five two-inch IVC9000 VTRs, three Ampex 200B VTRs, Ampex HS100C Video disc recorder, two Vital switchers, telecine, several colour cameras and the necessary supporting video and audio equipment. The VTRs and mixers have interfaces to a PDP11/34 computer to allow for computer-assisted editing. A new mixer will soon be installed that will have digital mixing control and event memory of our own design. The IVC9000 recorders have been modified for a 700 millisecond lockup and the unique capability of recording one frame at a time for animation.

The Video Center is connected to the Computer Graphics Lab by a multichannel CATV system. Both digital and video signals can be passed between the two centres and it is possible for the Computer Graphics Lab to control the video equipment in the Video Center.

3. Computer Graphics Lab Hardware

The major pieces of equipment in the Graphics Lab are:

Framebuffers. Each framebuffer is a 512 x 512 byte memory with a video port and an interface to computers which allow random access. Thus, a framebuffer can store a colour picture which an artist can observe while using computer programs to modify the picture. We have a total of 22 framebuffers: 6 from Evans and Sutherland, 12 from Genisco, and 4 from DeAnza. Framebuffers may be allocated in threes to give 8 bits each for red, green and blue components. The framebuffers are the focal point of the software in the lab. All images to be recorded are assembled in the framebuffers.

Computers. We have a VAX 11/780, PDP 11/70, 11/45, seven 11/34's, and various 11/35's and 11/04's for special functions. The 11/70 is our central time-sharing machine. The VAX is a production recording machine which assembles pictures into framebuffers. The 11/45 is devoted to real-time line drawing hardware. The 11/34's each have an 88 megabyte disc, a real-time refresh vector display and tablet. They are used as stand-alone graphics stations for artists and researchers.

Scanner. The DeAnza framebuffers have a unique processor that digitizes a video signal and performs frame-time image processing in the resulting digital image. There is also a slower video digitizer from Spatial Data for scanning in still artwork.

Film recorder. We have a Dicomed D48 colour film recorder. With this we can record the contents of framebuffers on to 35mm movie film with high precision.

Video recorder. There is an IVC9000 VTR (in addition to the five in the Video Center) which is capable of single frame recording and is under the control of the 11/70.

Line drawing displays. For real-time interactive 3D graphics we have Evans and Sutherland Picture Systems I and II. For 2D graphics we use the Three Rivers GDP which is capable of drawing an immense number of short vectors. There are also six Tektronix 4014's for less demanding applications.

Other. We have digitizing tablets, Barco monitors, and other typical support equipment.

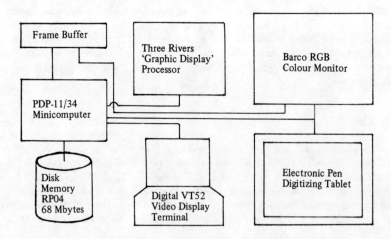

4. Software

Over the past four years the staff of the Computer Graphics Lab has developed several proprietary software systems and programs to use the various items of equipment to make animated sequences.

PAINT. This system allows an artist to paint using a pen and tablet and watching a colour TV monitor. Developed by Dr Alvy Ray Smith, the PAINT system is versatile and easy to use. It is in full-time use by artists who have no technical training. They are able to control a virtual paint brush in position, colour and size, and have several commands to call on: PICTURE – this enables the artist to paint a simple element and then place multiple copies of that element at different points in the picture. For example, in creating a forest background, a small clump of leaves can be drawn and then distributed over the branches of the trees. Some leaves would probably be drawn individually to avoid a repeated pattern. FILTER – this allows shading. There are also SMEAR, SLIDE and ZOOM. By using these commands as needed, artists can generate background images much faster without limiting or changing their individual painting styles.

SCAN-AND-PAINT. The drawings of conventional animation are normally copied onto acetate and coloured by hand. Dr Garland Stern has developed a system called SCAN-AND-PAINT where the drawings are scanned into a framebuffer, painted with the aid of a computer, merged onto backgrounds painted with the PAINT system, and recorded directly onto videotape or film. It takes less than one second to scan an original drawing, do whatever image enhancement is needed, and store the image. Colouring is done by sliding the pen over the tablet until the cursor on the screen moves onto a selected colour on a 'palette' along the bottom of the screen. After pressing the spring-loaded pen on the tablet at that point, the artist moves the cursor into the enclosed space in the character that is to be painted and there presses the electronic pen again. The desired colour immediately fills the space on the monitor, and the artist goes on to the next space. The TINT-FILL module in the package eliminates aliasing (also known as staircasing or 'jaggies') that has been a problem with computer-assisted colour filling of character images.

TWEEN. A system called TWEEN has been written wherein drawings that have been traced in can be played back in real time, coloured automatically, and for simple figures, intermediate drawings can be created from extreme poses. This system was written by Dr Edwin Catmull. The artists enters extremes which provide the computer with the necessary graphic information to generate automatically the in-betweens. In other words, the computer interpolates shapes and positions on the extreme drawings to determine what the intermediate images should look like.

UTILITIES. There is a large body of special effects routines for generating pans, zooms, blurring, highlights, distortions, etc. Several high quality commercials have been created using these routines.

THREE-DIMENSIONAL OBJECTS. Programs have been developed for displaying images of three-dimensional objects made of polygons, ellipsoids, and bicubic patches. The objects can be manipulated in real time on a Picture System or rendered as solid surfaces into framebuffers. A software package called TEXAS (written by Alvy Ray Smith) composes 3D images by electronically arranging units of scenery like flats on a stage. The artist can place background flats at any angle to the plane of the frame so as to give a realistic impression of depth.

5. The Artist and the Computer

While we have stressed to artists that the computer is nothing more than a new tool, some have felt threatened. When they use the programs some have tried unsuccessfully to make the computer do exactly what they do on paper. Others have embraced the new tools and quickly produced polished and satisfying images.

Some of the artists who use the system have no technical background at all and do not need it. The goal for any software put into production is that an artist be able to use it naturally with minimal training and only need go to an operator for assistance if required.

6. Current Research

Research is progressing in several key areas.

3D. A major effort is directed towards the creation, manipulation and rendering of 3D data bases so that images appear realistic. These techniques make possible some powerful tools for storytelling.

Scanning. At times our system is used as if it were a 'digital optical printer'. We must, of course, be able to scan in images from film or videotape with minimum loss of image quality. This requires precision equipment, compensation programs for any intensity nonlinearities or illumination variation, and image enhancement programs.

Faster processing. While digital processing is very general, it is sometimes slow. We are currently building a very fast microprogrammable processor/framebuffer system. One important criterion for the processor is that it be easy to program.

Sound. Digital audio equipment has just been acquired to go with an array processor (Floating Point System AP120-B) to give us a capability for digital synthesis and manipulation of sound.

7. Summary

By using the digital framebuffer and the general purpose computer we have put together an imagemaking system with great capability. The NYIT system of hardware and software has been successfully used to make an animated film, some commercials, and animated sequences to demonstrate the power and versatility of the system. We have been able to produce some astonishing results.

CADCENTRE

Computer Aided Design Centre
Madingley Road
Cambridge
CB3 0HB
England

Telephone: 0223 63125
Telex: 81420

Contact: Gordon Freeman.

Contents

1. Introduction
2. Hardware
3. Basic Software
4. Applications Software
5. The Future

1. Introduction

CADCENTRE is a Department of Industry Industrial Research Establishment sited at Cambridge. Founded in 1968 with the evangelistic task of spreading the gospel of Computer Aided Design (CAD) amongst British Industry, CADCENTRE has expanded and broadened its horizons to its current position as a world-renowned authority on CAD and Computer Aided Manufacture (CAM).

Although the majority of the CADCENTRE's staff of 150 are concerned with the production of advanced software, two particular groups should be mentioned in the context of this chapter: these are the Hardware Development Group and the Production Services Unit.

The Hardware Development Group has evolved from the need to build interfaces and displays where none was available on the market: recently (1979) this has been formalised, and a profit-centre manager appointed, in order that developments may be undertaken on behalf of clients and that existing products may be effectively presented in the market place.

The Production Services Unit exists to take on work for clients who may have no computers of their own or lack expertise in their use. The work undertaken by this group may vary from laying out printed circuit boards to producing all the drawing and Numerical Control (NC) tapes for machining a ship's propeller. Recently the Production Services Unit has acquired a three-axis milling machine which has been used for the production of models and components varying from a boat-hull to turbine blades. In short this group will take on almost any job, on behalf of a client, in the areas of draughting, NC systems and visualization.

2. Hardware

The hardware used by CADCENTRE for image making varies from pen-plotters through storage tubes and refresh displays to raster-scan colour displays and the NC machine-tool mentioned above. The reader will be familiar with the range of plotters and storage-tube displays available, so this section will concentrate upon the display hardware developed at the CADCENTRE and describe the particular facilities available on that.

The AGDT-Bugstore was developed at Cambridge as a tool for advanced visualization and film-making. At the heart of the display is a frame-buffer which holds a digital representation of the picture displayed on a colour television monitor. The logic of the Bugstore is designed so that the resolution of the displayed picture may be traded off against the number of colours available. Thus the frame-store, which is nominally 32K of 48-bit words may be used to display pictures in four different modes:

Mode	Picture Resolution (X by Y)	Number of Colours
3-bit	1024 x 512	8
6-bit	512 x 512	64
12-bit	256 x 512	4096
24-bit	128 x 512	>16.5 million

In 3-bit and 6-bit mode the colours are chosen from a colour-map which is 24 bits wide and 64 words long, thus enabling the user to choose any 8 or 64 colours respectively. In 12-bit and 24-bit mode the colours are written directly into the frame store. In both these cases the colours are stored in terms of their relative Red, Green, and Blue contents and thus used to drive the respective guns on the TV monitor via digital-to-analogue converters.

Of the four modes available, the most used is 6-bit mode which offers a very good compromise between picture resolution and colour selection. This mode allows the user to produce shaded pictures of a high quality with the minimum of jagged edges on non-orthogonal boundaries: however, scenes constructed from more than about four different materials, which correspond to bands of colour, can be difficult and for this reason experiments are currently being carried out using 12-bit and 24-bit mode. The results so far are very pleasing and interesting effects have been created simulating multiple multicoloured light-sources, shining onto objects with varying reflective qualities.

3-bit mode has been used for film-making in the past, with particular reference to animation of data derived from complex traffic simulations. In these cases the application does not call for a large number of colours but resolution is important in order that a relatively cluttered scene may be distinctly displayed.

The Bugstore is interfaced to the host-computer via a 16-bit parallel link which runs at up to 10 megabits per second. In theory this enables the entire frame buffer to be overwritten in less than 1 second, but in practice the host machine cannot supply data at this rate. The speed at which pictures change must therefore depend upon what application is being run, and which computer is being used as a host. At the time of writing Bugstore has been interfaced to Prime 300 and 400 machines, PDP-11/70 and PDP11/34's.

However, there is no reason to assume that this list should be considered restrictive: Bugstore is designed to be machine independent and should be applicable to any machine with a 16-bit parallel interface available. All the basic driving software is written in FORTRAN which means that implementation onto foreign hosts may be carried out with the minimum of trouble.

Other hardware available for graphics at CADCENTRE is of less esoteric design, though is no less useful for that. For the sake of completeness the list below should suffice to indicate the range of facilities:

. Calcomp drum plotters (30" width)
. Calcomp 748 flat-bed plotter
. Konigsberg Kingmatic Draughting Machine (with photo-head for artwork)
. Tektronix storage tubes (4006, 4010, 4014)
. Imlac PDS-1 refresh display

3. Basic Software

CADCENTRE has long realised that its software must be machine-independent in order to be competitive. For this reason basic graphics software has been developed for use in a wide variety of applications on a broad spectrum of computers.

Perhaps the best known, and certainly the most widely used (c. 200 sites), of CAD-CENTRE's products is GINO-F. This is a library of FORTRAN routines for line-drawing applications. The routines are designed in such a way that the user may, if he wishes, write a program using GINO-F which will be independent both of host machine and graphics device. However, the user may also make use of the most advanced facilities available on modern hardware via the GINO-F interface. GINO-F has a complete range of 3-dimensional routines which allow the user to draw solid objects with a number of different projections and with or without perspective.

There are other packages in the so-called GINO-family which enable the user to write programs in particular application areas with minimum effort. These are GINOGRAF for drawing graphs, histograms, bar-charts and pie charts, GINOZONE for displaying zonal based data (e.g. population or rainfall maps), GINOSURF which is used for producing contoured data and representations of complex surfaces and finally GINO-2D which is a two-dimensional sub-set of GINO-F which has been rewritten entirely in order to remove the overheads in both program size and speed which are necessary in the 3-dimensional package.

GINO is designed as a line-drawing package and is therefore not ideal for use with the Bugstore which is best applied to applications involving area-filling and shaded picture representation (however, a GINO driver for Bugstore is available should it be required). For this reason a special set of low-level routines have been developed which are known as BUTIL and enable the user to write programs for Bugstore using a small number of primitive shapes (lines, discs, orthogonal rectangles, polygons and quadrilaterals). BUTIL also contains all the necessary routines for initialization of the Bugstore and control of the colour-map and housekeeping operations.

Between them GINO and BUTIL allow a user to build programs which will produce graphics for almost any application: we will now discuss some of the areas in which they have been applied by CADCENTRE for image-making.

4. Applications Software

For the purposes of this section I propose to sub-divide the software into two categories: visualization software where the application is concerned with aesthetics and what a thing looks like, and draughting software which concerns engineering drawings and their accurate interpretation. In some cases they may overlap as both parts are inherent in the design process.

In the visualization area the two most important programs are GREYSCALES and HID-DEN LINES. These programs allow the user to display shaded pictures and drawings of 3-D models on the Bugstore and line drawing devices respectively. Both programs are run interactively and allow the user to build up a scene from various component models and view it from any direction with any, or no, perspective. This has been applied to a wide variety of applications from the visualization of finite element mesh data as a means of data checking to visualization of street scenes, NC models, photomontage of new roads and bridges, and chemical plants. GREYSCALES also allows the user to apply different material types to the surfaces to give the effect of, for instance, glass or paper or concrete. Furthermore GREYSCALES allows the user to position a light source at infinite distance in any direction.

However, in order to view these models they must first be generated. This may be done in a variety of ways, but the most important are via THINGS and POLYSURF. THINGS (Three dimensional

INput of Graphical Solids) is a library of FORTRAN routines which enables the user to define an object in terms of primitive solids such as cubes, cylinders, frustra and bounded planes. This system is ideal when the required scene is largely made up of orthogonal objects, but is not suitable for doubly-curved surfaces. In this case POLYSURF is the system favoured by CADCENTRE. In broad terms the model is constructed by fitting a curved surface around a number of pre-determined cross-sections and is ideal for such objects as boat-hulls, shoe-lasts and turbine blades.

The last system to be covered by this report in the area of visualization is an interactive sketching program for the Bugstore which is based upon BUTIL, the basic software package. Interactive BUTIL, as this system is known, allows the user to transfer a sketch held on a Tablet, or digitizer, to the Bugstore screen and to colour the resulting picture and modify it as it is created. This has applications in the area of designing logos, advertising material and cartoon animation. This last area is particularly relevant as the system allows the user to create two pictures which may be related or totally dissimilar, and to generate intermediate frames which convert from one key-frame to the next. Another similar system has been developed for carpets or fabric pattern design where a high degree of pattern repetition may be present.

Draughting software tends to have one major difference from visualization software in that the graphics produced by the program are usually a bi-product of a larger engineering system rather than the end-product. The graphics also tend to be line-drawing rather than shaded pictures.

The first area covered is the area of NC systems whereby a component may be defined either in 2 dimensions for an object to be turned on a lathe or in 2½ dimensions for an object to be cut on a 3-axis machine. The user may then interactively program the machine-tool movements to cut the component and watch these movements being traced out on a storage-tube screen and check for errors. Finally an NC control tape is produced for component manufacture. POLYSURF (see above) may be considered as the full 3-D part of these systems and is indeed designed as an NC system rather than a modelling system.

Another area covered by CADCENTRE is that of pipe-routing in chemical-plant design. PDMS is a very large suite of programs, and one of the bi-products is a comprehensive system for production of perspective and working drawings of the plant.

In the general draughting area CADCENTRE·has a number of facilities varying from a simple schematic drawing system to full-blown draughting systems with database back-up which are comparable with large turnkey systems.

In summary, it may be fairly said that whatever application a user may have for computer graphics, CADCENTRE has probably looked at it, and if CADCENTRE does not have a suitable product, then it may well be interested in producing one.

5. The Future

CADCENTRE needs to be looking ahead continually and this report would not be complete without a little crystal-ball gazing.

The Hardware Group are developing a new graphics display which is designed for the image-processing market, in particular for analysing images from scanning electron microscopes and satellites. New developments are going on all the time in the area of advanced visualization software and modelling systems, some of which was mentioned above.

Overall, the reader should be aware that all work at CADCENTRE is customer-oriented and so the future work of the Centre will be based upon the demands of the customers.

COMPUTER IMAGE CORPORATION

CIC
2475 West Second Avenue
Suite 4
Denver
Colorado 80223
USA

Telephone: (303) 934-5801

Contact: Ed Tajchman
                Vice President, Engineering

Contents:

1. Introduction

Animate multiple characters in full colour with lip sync over a painted or live background and see the finished scene the same day? Impossible! Well, it may have been impossible a few years ago but not any more. Electronic animation systems developed by Computer Image Corporation enable a producer to do just that.

These electronic animation systems, Scanimate®, CAESAR and soon the System IV, employ a mapping technique that requires only artwork and some instructions from the animation director to produce the desired animation. Usually the instructions will be verbal. "That title should be a little larger and make the red a little brighter" or "the Tiger's tail should twitch more on that beat. Try making it a little longer and make it move a little faster". Statements like these are how a director controls the animation in production. The animation can be judged as it is produced because it is displayed in either real time or slow motion playback on a television monitor.

An animator/operator will respond to the verbal instructions by manipulating the animation system's controls to produce the requested change in the image. Within seconds the director will know if his changes have created the desired effect in the animation. The animation can be viewed in full colour and decisions made if any other changes are necessary. This is possible because Computer Image's animation systems have certain features that make them very powerful tools. With them, an animator can see the final results of his imagination within hours or days instead of the usual weeks or months.

One key feature of these systems is the method of using artwork as the input and storage medium for the detailed image information. The artwork can be stored on a piece of film or in a digital frame store memory. Many computer animation systems claim that only the ideas that exist in the artist's mind are required to produce animation. However, a computer cannot read an artist's mind. In some manner, the details of the imagined scene must be communicated to the system as it can only work with the data given to it. The artist might be able to create the punched cards, magnetic tape or use some other means of digital communication to program the image into the system. However, artists are usually not programmers. They express their ideas best with pictures drawn with pencils as they were traditionally trained to do.

When an artist draws a logo, a symbol or a figure, it is that image that he or she wishes to animate. Pure digital computer animation systems require a programmer to extract the details of the image and arrange them into the proper form for the computer. Even then, it can be very difficult to communicate all of the important characteristics of the image to the system as the programmer may not appreciate the fine points of the artist's drawings. Also, an artist may not draw in a manner that is easily transferred by mathematical equations. If the image cannot be described by equations, then a point by point description may be necessary. This type of interface between the artist and the computer is tedious and time consuming at best and then may not be satisfactory. Since the artist will usually draw the desired image anyway to describe it to the programmer, then it is advantageous to use the drawing directly to program the image.

2. Operation of system

The drawing is prepared for the animation system's input by an artist who first dismembers the character so that each portion of the character that is to move independently of any other portion is drawn in an isolated view. These isolated portions are arranged vertically and converted by a photographic process to high contrast artwork.

Colour coding is achieved by assigning different values of grey scale material to clear areas that are to have independent colours. The animation system discriminates each particular shade of grey and an operator can assign any colour to that area. Areas with different grey scales can have different or identical colours. Different grey scales merely identify areas whose colours can be arbitrarily selected. This means that colour can be changed during a sequence. A particular shade of grey can be coded to be red at the beginning of a scene, jump to blue at some time and then shift to yellow by the end of the sequence.

A CAESAR feature is the operation of a subsystem called 'Overlap'. This system provides a real-time solution to the hidden line problem. It makes it possible for a character to move an arm in front of its face without producing image interference where the two sections overlap.

A method of controlled a blanking window applied to the input video makes it possible to have seven mouths, displaced horizontally, drawn on one section but to have only the chosen one visible on the composed character. Since the blanking parameters are controllable, the operator can display any particular mouth on any specific frame. This feature can be used with any and all of the sections containing the character's features so that a clenched fist can be substituted for an open hand, a side view for a frontal view of a head, etc.

To produce an animated sequence, the animator first composes the necessary key frames directly on the system by varying the control parameters. Size, shape, position, centre and angle of rotation and colour of each grey scale coded portion of the character are some of the independently controllable parameters. First the desired parameter must be selected. Then the parameter value can be varied by turning a knob and the effect viewed on a television monitor. Instant visual feedback helps the animator decide the optimum parameter values needed to create the correct key frame.

On the CAESAR system up to eight key frames, with the animator specifying the time interval between them, can be constructed at one time. These key frames can be checked for relative positions by instantly recalling and viewing them, 'flipping key frames'. After the animator has reviewed the key frames, modifying them when necessary, and is satisfied with them he pushes a button to let CAESAR proceed to compute the 'Inbetweens'. The video frames between the key frames are now filled in by the computer. In just seconds the acton is ready to view.

The Scanimate® system uses two key frames as its method of animation generation. They are usually called the 'initial' and 'final' frames. Each of these frames can be carefully composed by the operator who can also control some selectable parameters at several intermediate intervals.

The Scanimate® system is basically a graphics animation device with output imagery that can surprise the operator due to the system's analogue nature. CAESAR will produce animation exactly as specified by the control settings so it is very powerful when the director knows exactly what animation is desired. When these two systems are operated in tandem, each with its special strengths, then a very powerful animation production facility exists. Video productions created within this facility run the gamut from startling abstract effects used in television commercials, to full character animation useful in all types of productions, and on to the precise graphic manipulation useful for industrial training. To demonstrate the different steps normally taken to complete a production, a typical job will be described.

Production usually begins with a storyboard which is very similar to a comic strip. Each panel of the storyboard illustrates the key visual elements present in a particular scene. It is drawn by an artist who takes a concept and determines the images and movement that will best project it. After the storyboard is approved by both the director and the client, the process continues with the generation of a script. A sound track is then produced from the script at a sound studio where the different voices, sound effects and music are all mixed and recorded on magnetic tape. If the production is to include lip sync, the sound track must be 'read'. The result of this process are bar sheets that indicate the precise time at which each syllable of each spoken word occurs. During this time, an artist/animator can analyze the storyboard and generate the artwork required to produce the animation. Several different backgrounds may be required and are prepared in full colour. The animated characters for each scene are then prepared as grey scaled artwork. At least one piece of input artwork is required for each scene. If several characters are involved in the scene then a separate piece of artwork may be required for each of them.

3. Production of animation

Now the actual production of animation can begin. A scene is selected and the proper artwork set into place. Grey scaled artwork defining the animated character is used as the system input. Full colour art scanned by a colour TV camera, video from a VTR or another animation system output can be the background video.

An animator now creates an animated sequence by building a series of key frames using the technique previously discussed. The director has an opportunity to control the animation by inserting himself into the feedback process. Lip sync can now be added by specifying which one of up to seven different mouth shapes should be used at the times specified by the bar sheet. The chosen mouth shape will be inserted onto the character and will track the animation already constructed. The sound track itself is used as a timing source.

After the director is satisfied with the completed animation, the sequence of the character keyed over the background video is recorded on videotape. If more than one character is desired, additional characters can be keyed over the composite scene in successive passes. A single scene can contain from one to ten or more passes. This process continues until all of the scenes required for the production have been recorded on videotape.

The production is completed by using videotape editing techniques to combine the many scenes together in the proper order. Two or three VTRs, a time code system and a modern television switcher are used for this process. After the editing process is complete the production is ready for use in videotape form.

Utilizing electronic animation has enabled many producers to reduce the time span required to complete an animated project significantly. Buzz Potamkin, Executive Producer from Perpetual

Motion Pictures, Inc., gave the time span of a conventionally animated 30 second television commercial to be 7 to 9 weeks on a normal schedule and 3 to 5 weeks on a rush schedule (Business Screen, July 1977). The normal schedule for an electronically animated 30 second spot is much shorter. There is no change in the time required for the Design and Track development stage which can take 3 working days. However the remaining phases — Layout, Animation, Ink and Paint, and Completion to tape — can all be shortened. A very limited amount of artwork must be prepared because of the animation technique used. Allowing 1 to 2 days to produce the animation electronically, then from concept to finished product, a total time span of from one to one and one half weeks for the production of a 30 second spot is reasonable.

4. Systems and hardware

The technology employed by Computer Image Corporation has been under development since 1956. Lee Harrison III started dreaming about automating the production of animation after receiving his degree in Fine Arts. He started the creation of such a system after acquiring an Engineering degree in 1959. Implementation of these ideas became the goal of Computer Image which he founded in 1967.

Since then, three major animation systems have been developed and patented; Animac, Scanimate® and CAESAR. Animac is the pioneer system using analogue computer technology and it generated great excitement and a few commercial productions. However, its programmability and image quality were not adequate for wide commercial use. All images were internally generated in two- or three-dimensional space.

Scanimate® is the second generation system. An Emmy was awarded in 1972 by the Television Academy for the development of Scanimate®. It has become a commercial success and is in operation at Computer Image Production in Denver, Image West in Hollywood, Dolphin Productions in New York City and at Far East Laboratories in Tokyo. The Scanimate® system is a hybrid, utilizing analogue computer and television technology in a mapping process to produce animation. Inclusion of a digital computer in CAESAR makes operating it simpler, enables precise timing and positioning of the animation and the production of long sequences.

A complete, state-of-the-art, electronic, animation facility is operated by Computer Image Corporation in Denver, Colorado, U.S.A. Scanimate® and CAESAR are the names of the two systems that are the core of the facility. These sytems are supported by a complement of trained artists, animators, directors and engineers as well as by all of the standard television equipment normally required for video production.

The support equipment features two International Video Corporation (IVC) model 9000 videotape recorders (VTRs). These VTRs are the best quality ever built and are used to master the animated material. There is also one standard quadruplex VTR, an Ampex 1200B, that is used to communicate with the television industry. A colour camera is available to incorporate full colour backgrounds or live action with the animation. All of the video sources can be combined with the use of a switcher, a Computer Image Video Controller. There are also several panning devices that move black and white or full colour artwork under computer control.

All of these systems are intergrated through the use of a micro-processor based Automation controller. This controller enables the synchronization of the various pieces of equipment, usually with respect to a starting signal derived from the SMPTE time code contained on the video tape being played back by one of the VTRs. The timing between a series of events can be programmed, rehearsed to see if the desired effects are achieved and then modified until everything is satisfactory.

5. Staff support and costing

Computer Image's production facility include directors who can create a storyboard that will portray a concept or idea dynamically. The directors can then if necessary also design the characters – symbols, logos etc., to be animated and then direct the actual animation process. They are supported by an art staff that can convert drawings of the characters into high contrast, grey scaled artwork properly positioned on acetate cels ready for the animation system. They can also create the full colour background art often used in a video production.

The price for a finished animated production is based on a number of variables which are dependent on the complexity of the production. Some of the variables are: The number of characters or moving symbols, the number of colours and amount of detail in the animated characters, whether lip sync is required, the number of scenes and the type of transitions to be used between scenes.

All of these variables affect the price because they help determine the amount of animation system time required to complete the production. A director will examine the information from the prospective client which, ideally, is a storyboard prepared by someone familiar with the Computer Image animation techniques. The director will make the best estimate possible of the time required and a price determined at the rate of $7,000 U.S. dollars per eight hour animation shift, this estimate is reviewed by the production manager and the resulting amount is then submitted as a fixed price bid for the agreed upon production. The day rate includes the full use of the equipment in the production facility and the associated operators, the art staff and a staff director. Productions that involve an extraordinary usage of video tape, special art preparation or animation direction may require extra charges that are agreed upon before the actual production. Other services that can be provided for extra charge include script writing, sound track production and transferring the animation from videotape to film.

Some productions that do not have a critical finish date may be bid for production at a negotiable R.O.S. (Run of Schedule) rate that is more favourable to the customer. These productions are at times convenient to the production facility and so usually require a longer time interval for completion. Production contracts at reduced bulk rates for a significant amount of production time that must be scheduled within a specified time interval, usually one year, are also available.

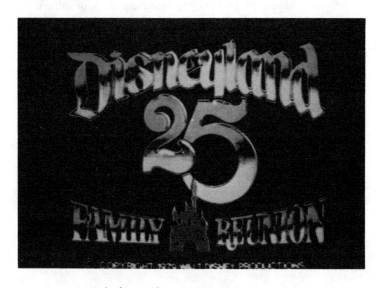

Single frame of animated logo for Disneyland.

COMPUTER GRAPHICS IN EDUCATION AND RESEARCH

The remaining two chapters consider the application of computer imagemaking to teaching and research. Here, the emphasis is not so much on the images themselves but rather on the use to which comparatively simple images can be put. The use of computers in education is now widespread and there is considerable interest in computer-assisted learning (CAL). In recent years there has been a major effort expended in trying to apply the techniques of interactive imagemaking to the teaching of science.

At the conference on Computers for Imagemaking (April 1978) from which this book has developed, Dr Diana Laurillard of the University of Surrey, Institute for Educational Technology, presented a paper on the use of interactive computer graphics in science teaching. This work was part of a major national project, the National Development Programme in Computer Assisted Learning (NDPCAL) directed by Richard Hooper. The scope and achievements of this project have been published in **Interactive Computer Graphics in Science Teaching** edited by McKenzie, Elton and Lewis, and this book is a valuable introduction to this fast-growing field.

The main thrust of the graphical side of this programme was the visualisation of the mathematical descriptions that underly scientific thought. If this visualisation could be made interactive, then, it is argued, all the merits of the 'discovery method' of learning can be adapted to theoretical explorations. The programs that provide the data for display are, however, determinate. The student explores the effects of changing parameters or boundary conditions in fixed equations that are known and appropriate.

This is not the strategy underlying the work reported on in Chapter 6. Here, Professor Hazony is trying to extend the systems of computation to allow for the generation of 'new' expressions in the search for a solution to a particular problem.

The following chapter, by Dr John Richmond and Dr John Gilbert, is a case-study that sets out to expose the underlying strategies in the design of images for teaching. The lessons they adduce apply not just to the batch computation of images for mathematical programmes but to all cases where images are required.

PROBLEM SOLVING ON A CENTRALIZED
INTERACTIVE COMPUTER GRAPHICS SYSTEM

Yehonathan Hazony

Princeton University

A centralized interactive computer graphics system for general purpose problem solving is described. The system was developed at Princeton University and is used for applications in the natural sciences, engineering and management. Design philosophy and performance are discussed and demonstrated.

The fast developing field of interactive computer graphics now offers excellent production tools in the areas of education, design, production, distribution and management. These tools are sufficiently powerful to counteract the increasing pressures exerted on industry by the constraints of limited resources. These pressures have a direct impact on contemporary engineering education, by adding new disciplines to be mastered. The teaching of these novel subjects needs time and so competes with classical foundations for the limited time and resources available to the engineering student. The power and flexibility of the interactive computer graphics system at Princeton University described in the present chapter, have been developed with the prime objective of providing the undergraduate students with new ways of thinking productively about the kinds of problems they will encounter in the industrial and business market place after graduation. However, they have also helped them to cope with an ever increasing curricular load.

The rapid developments in computer technology and its application to industry and commerce open the door for the introduction of interactive computer graphics on a similarly large scale. However, the vast expansion and proliferation of digital computers pose a new severe problem for the allocation of limited resources. This time the limit is to the human resources available to support such a proliferation. It is clear that the traditional approach, where a digital computer is supported by dedicated specialized personnel, is giving way to the mode of operation where often hundreds of mini-computers are supported by a centralized network in turn supported by a comparatively small number of people. Even installations with powerful centralized large scale computers have difficulties in maintaining the traditional level of technical support. This lack of qualified personnel is forcing their rapid substitution by systems which do not require such an extensive technical support.

Computer technology is developing as a powerful tool for problem solving in engineering, science and management. However, in the contention over manpower, the computer field cannot lure more than a subset of the available pool of engineering students. Consequently, the methodology of interactive computer graphics has to develop in the direction of a general purpose tool for problem solving, to be used by professionals who are experts in disciplines other than the computer, which does

87

not require the help of a computer expert to use it. Furthermore, under the developing curricular pressures in all disciplines of engineering, it is clear that most engineering graduates may not be required to take more than one introductory course to computers and computing, and yet they need to be able to make very effective use of this technology.

The engineering field is developing in a dangerous direction. It will soon be dominated by the use of computers, but will lack the support of the human resources which were once available for each computer installation when computers were scarce and expensive. Consequently, the appropriate methodology has to be developed as well as the technical aptitudes of the respective professionals.

Guidelines for the development of the appropriate computer methodology may be derived by going back to the days prior to the digital computer, where the combined use of graphics and applied mathematics played an undisputed key role in engineering. It is therefore reasonable to expect the future generation of engineers to be equipped with graphical perception as well as high aptitude for mathematics and mathematical notation.

If the new generation of computers are to be integrated smoothly into the evolution of the fields of engineering then using computer graphics must become as easy as using the drafting board, and using the analytical powers offered by the digital machine should not exceed the intellectual challenge of writing a mathematical expression on the blackboard or in a notebook.

However, the integration of the computer into the process should offer the advantage of immediate execution. That is, modified graphical design may be instantly turned into a final drawing, and the writing of a conceptual mathematical expression be followed by an immediate quantitative evaluation. This combination meets the needs of contemporary engineering design. Here, mathematical modelling is to be used in the iterative design process, supporting human intuition by quantitative analysis, in the convergence towards a final design product.

THE PROBLEM-SOLVING ENVIRONMENT

Many problems have a common initial state: data is available which indicates that there is a need for a solution to a problem, but the problem itself is poorly specified. A medical doctor sees the symptoms of a possible disease but cannot prescribe the medication before going through the diagnostics stage. Similarly, a structural engineer can easily recognise the fact that a dome has collapsed over a stadium, but that recognition does not mean he understands the structural problem that he has to solve. Similar examples can probably be given for any discipline. It is impossible to apply rigid analytical methods to solve vaguely-defined problems. Therefore, the initial stage may be regarded as an exploratory one, which is often addressed via an attempt to search through the available data for a possible clue to the nature of the problem. This early stage in problem-solving may be characterized as the problem definition stage.

Since the proper definition of the problem at hand is the most critical component in the solution process, it would be worthwhile to design the computer system to be useful at this early stage. The exploratory nature of the analysis gives a tremendous advantage to an interactive system, that is, a system which responds instantly, permitting the analyst to interact with the process and interject into it his intuitive judgement. Furthermore, in situations where the problem definition process requires the exploration of a large volume of data, the flexibility of interactive pictorial analysis becomes very powerful.

The interactive graphical system must be capable of handling the large volume of data required by a pictorial data analysis system and be fast enough not to disrupt the continuity of thought of the analyst. This is a flexible requirement which depends on the kind of problem at hand and the stage of the solution process. The response time expected by the analyst varies according to the stage at which it is working. In the initial explorations, it is common to expect a response time of less than a second, but as the analysis proceeds, the time intervals between new ideas become longer, and a longer response time is tolerable. This is consistent with the fact that at this point the analyst's ideas are more sophisticated and typically require longer execution time.

A better insight into the nature of the problem to be solved leads to an attempt at the second stage of the process, which is that of **solution formulation**. At this stage the actual solution algorithm or procedure is formulated for a defined problem. An effective interactive system will permit the analyst to iterate back and forth between the stages of problem definition and solution formulation. This may lead to further refinement of the definition of the problem prior to the actual solution process.

The next stage would be the **numerical solution** stage, where the digital computer is unleashed, with the required strength, to follow the formulated solution algorithm to provide answers to what hopefully are the right questions.

The final stage in the process is that of **reporting and documentation**. This is a much-neglected stage, but it is as important as all the others. For a solution to a problem in any discipline to have any value or meaning, the results must be communicated in order for them to be implemented. Furthermore, a lack of adequate documentation makes it impossible for future recipients of the results to go back and validate them, if necessary, or to build upon them in future extensions of the work. This may mean that somebody might have to go back and redo the project from scratch, if the results are to be considered as accurate enough to become the foundation of an implementation for future extensions of the study. The stage of reporting and documentation is often more tedious and time-consuming than the solution process, and this is definitely an area where the powers of the digital computer may be put to extremely valuable use.

An important facet of the problem-solving process is the fluctuation in the extent to which the digital machine is used in the different stages. Depending on the nature of the problem, one may or may not resort to extensive computer power in the initial exploratory problem-definition stage. The solution-formulation stage may require more work with pencil and paper than with the machine, while the final solution stage typically requires most of the computer power. The documentation stage could take advantage of word processing capabilities, which provide extensive facilities at a very small cost in machine time. These fluctuations in the role and extent of use of the digital computer are an important consideration in the system optimization process.

THE INTERACTIVE ENVIRONMENT

The term 'Interactive Computer Graphics' is used by different authors to mean different things. One may distiguish two different classes of 'interactive computer graphics' environments. One refers to the 'Turn Key' systems, which typically address specialized applications through specially designed tools. In applying the Turn Key system, the user follows a prescribed procedure, addressing a well-defined problem and arriving at a product which has been well specified in advance. Many of the Turn Key systems are very powerful and extremely interactive, that is, they respond instantly to the input by the operator, who may use external sources of information to guide the computerized process. The external source of information may often be the operator's intuition.

At the other extreme one may find the general purpose systems, which by definition can not be described in terms of specific well-defined procedures towards a well-defined application and product. The interactive computer graphics environment developed at the Interactive Computer Graphics Laboratory (ICGL) at Princeton University addresses the domain of general purpose problem solving with a particular emphasis on the educational environment. One way to clarify the goals of the project as well as the terminology used would be through several examples. Since the predominant interface between the human operator and the computer is the keyboard, the basic measure for interactiveness may be related to the human proficiency at the electric typewriter. One would expect the machine to respond to a request before a single character is typed, which typically takes a fraction of a second, while a more sophisticated instruction may require one minute to type. Consequently, we will use one second as our basic performance measure. Furthermore, it is an empirical observation that a user may preserve his/her continuity of thoughts and patience for several minutes once the response of the computer starts developing on the graphical screen. This establishes the minute as a second dimension of reference.

The following illustrations are designed to show what may be accomplished by a user of the general purpose interactive computer graphics system at a cost of less than 1 second of computation (CPU) time, and less than a minute of actual waiting (clock) time for the termination of the display. The centralized computer used is an IBM 3033 under the VM370/CMS operating system.

Integrals and Derivatives.

As a first example consider the numerical implementation of integrals and derivatives (Ref. 1). Consider the function

$$y = e^{-x^2}$$

defined over the range $\geqslant 5 \leqslant x \leqslant 5$ at discrete intervals of 0.1. In order to appreciate the errors involved in numerical analysis, consider the evaluation of

$$\int(\frac{de^{-x^2}}{dx})\,dx$$

which should result in the original y function. The following instructions

```
X←(0.1×ι101)-5.1
Y←EXP-X*2
PLOT Y MINUS INTEG 1 DERIV Y VS X
```

produce Fig. 1. In order to separate typing time from response time the above instructions have been embedded in the program FIG1.

```
        ∇ FIG1
[1]     TIME
[2]     X←(0.1×ι101)-5.1
[3]     Y←EXP-X*2
[4]     PLOT Y MINUS INTEG 1 DERIV Y VS X
[5]     DRAW 0 0 100
[6]     ' '
[7]     TIME
[8]     USERS
        ∇
```

TIME IS 14:26:27 EST WEDNESDAY 04/02/80
CONNECT= 00:04:27 VIRTCPU= 000:00.28 TOTCPU= 000:00.96

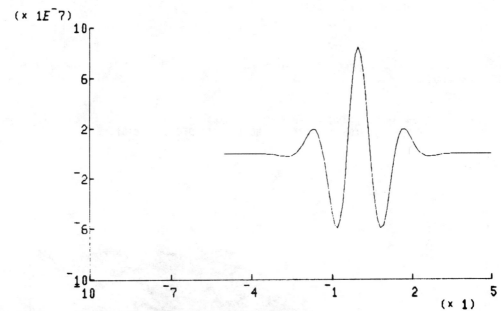

TIME IS 14:26:29 EST WEDNESDAY 04/02/80
CONNECT= 00:04:29 VIRTCPU= 000:00.39 TOTCPU= 000:01.13
095 USERS, 000 DIALED

Fig. 1. Numerical implementation of integrals and derivatives. The display of
$y - \int (dy/dx) dx$ indicates the magnitude of the errors introduced by the numerical
evaluation. The figures are reproduced from the screen of the Tektronix 4016 terminal.
The time stamps above and below provide a measure of the responsiveness of the system.
Also shown is the number of simultaneous users on the system at the end of the display.

The program includes time stamps before and after execution followed by the result of an inquiry as to
the number of simultaneous users on the system (line 8). The above program defines the argument x, evaluates the variable y, evaluates the first derivative of y with respect to x followed by the evaluation of the
integral and then a comparison with the original y. Finally the errors introduced through these numerical
procedures are automatically scaled and displayed graphically on the screen. The execution of this
program took 2 second of clock time from the time 'FIG1' was typed until the display was completed
at the cost of 0.15 seconds of CPU time.

Surfaces

The next example demonstrates the mathematical surface defined as

$Z = (SIN\ R) \div R$

This time the elapsed clock time includes the time required to type the instructions

```
X←(ι31)-16
R←(A∘.+A←X×2)*0.5
TRIPLOT (SIN R)÷R
```

which define the field of R prior to the corresponding display. Clock time here is about 1 minute and CPU time of 0.30 seconds.

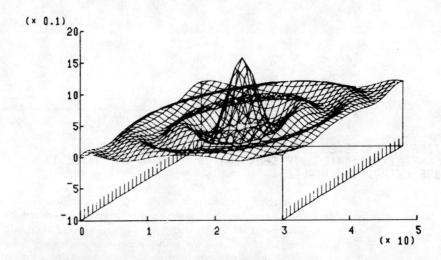

TIME IS 14:27:06 EST WEDNESDAY 04/02/80
CONNECT= 00:05:07 VIRTCPU= 000:00.41 TOTCPU= 000:01.17

TIME IS 14:27:22 EST WEDNESDAY 04/02/80
CONNECT= 00:05:22 VIRTCPU= 000:00.63 TOTCPU= 000:01.51
095 USERS, 000 DIALED

Fig. 2.   A three dimensional display of the mathematical surface (sin r) ÷ r. Generating the data and the display on the screen required 0.25 sec. of CPU time and 30 sec. of clock time due to large volume of data transmitted through a 4800 bds communication line.

Figure 3 illustrates the set of control points used to generate and display the surface patch shown in Fig. 4. These two figures illustrate the process of the computer generation of an arbitary surface (Ref. 2) at the costs of 0.25 seconds of CPU time and 20 seconds clock time.

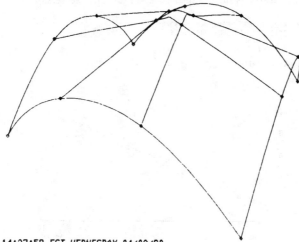

TIME IS 14:27:56 EST WEDNESDAY 04/02/80
CONNECT= 00:05:56 VIRTCPU= 000:00.65 TOTCPU= 000:01.56

TIME IS 14:27:59 EST WEDNESDAY 04/02/80
CONNECT= 00:05:59 VIRTCPU= 000:00.72 TOTCPU= 000:01.68
096 USERS, 000 DIALED

Fig. 3. A perspective view of 16 control points used to define the surface of a dome. Cardinal spline curves are shown to display the interrelations between the points.

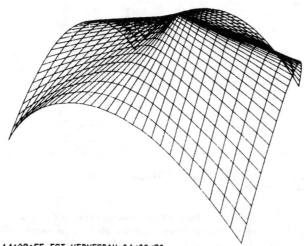

TIME IS 14:28:42 EST WEDNESDAY 04/02/80
CONNECT= 00:06:42 VIRTCPU= 000:00.94 TOTCPU= 000:02.03

TIME IS 14:28:55 EST WEDNESDAY 04/02/80
CONNECT= 00:06:56 VIRTCPU= 000:01.12 TOTCPU= 000:02.29
097 USERS, 000 DIALED

Fig. 4. A surface patch representing a dome. This surface is generated from the 16 control points shown in Fig. 3 using a perspective projection and spline interpolations at the costs of 0.25 sec. CPU time and about 30 sec. clock time.

Regression Analysis

Figure 5 illustrates the use of the system for linear regression.

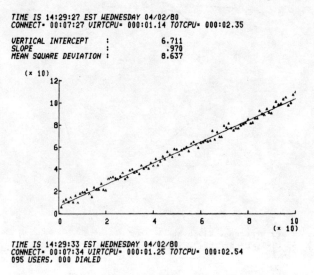

```
TIME IS 14:29:27 EST WEDNESDAY 04/02/80
CONNECT= 00:07:27 VIRTCPU= 000:01.14 TOTCPU= 000:02.35

VERTICAL INTERCEPT   :          6.711
SLOPE                :           .970
MEAN SQUARE DEVIATION :         8.637
```

```
TIME IS 14:29:33 EST WEDNESDAY 04/02/80
CONNECT= 00:07:34 VIRTCPU= 000:01.25 TOTCPU= 000:02.54
095 USERS, 000 DIALED
```

Fig. 5.   Linear regression fitting a linear model through a set of 'noisy' data.

```
TIME IS 14:30:06 EST WEDNESDAY 04/02/80
CONNECT= 00:08:06 VIRTCPU= 000:01.27 TOTCPU= 000:02.60
```

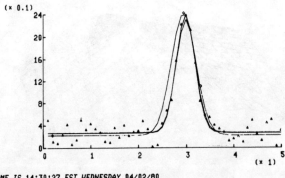

```
TIME IS 14:30:27 EST WEDNESDAY 04/02/80
CONNECT= 00:08:27 VIRTCPU= 000:01.47 TOTCPU= 000:02.92
093 USERS, 000 DIALED
```

Fig. 6.   Nonlinear regression fitting a Gaussian curve through a set of experimental resonance data. The nonlinear process starts with a set of initial estimates of the parameter entered from the screen of the terminal. These estimates are determined by a set of three points indicated by diamonds and the numbers, 1, 2 and 3. The y value of the first point provides an estimate for the baseline, the x and y coordinates of the second point indicate a guess at the centre position and resonance magnitude and the x value for the 3rd point indicates the location for the e^{-1} value. A poor choice of initial estimates was deliberately made to demonstrate the convergence of the process. The third and fourth iterations may not be distinguished visually.

Figure 6 demonstrates the nonlinear regression process of fitting the function

$$y = a + b \times e^{-(\frac{x-x_0}{c})^2}$$

to a given set of data, using the screen for input of the initial estimates for a, b, c and x_0. The fit shown is obtained at the fourth iteration at the costs of 0.3 seconds of CPU time and one minute clock time, which includes the times to enter the initial estimates. A poor set of initial estimates was deliberately chosen to demonstrate graphically the convergence of the iterative process.

Interactive Cartography

Figure 7 is taken from the domain of interactive cartography (Ref. 3).

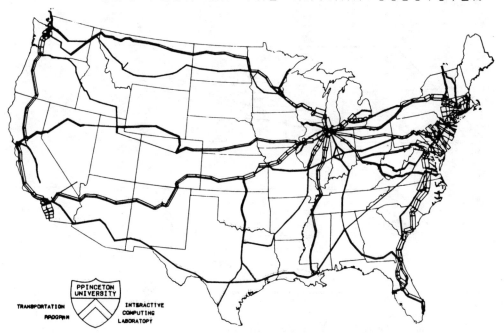

PASSENGER FLOW ON THE AMTRAK SUBSYSTEM

Fig. 7. The political and water boundaries of the USA and flow analysis on the Amtrak passenger system. This display contains about 10,000 vectors and takes about one minute of clock time to transmit at 4800 bds communication. This geopolitical data base provides the background for the display of the results of network flow analysis.

A newly emerging field in computer methodology is commonly referred to as 'Management Delivery Systems'. One key element in such systems is a fast way for analyzing the flow of information going upwards in a large corporation or a government agency for the purpose of a policy decision. The example relates to issues addressed by management in a major railroad corporation or a government agency like the Federal Railroad Administration (FRA) or the Interstate Commerce Commission (ICC). A typical study requires some background information like the political and water boundaries of the United States, which are shown in Fig. 7. The figure includes an additional overlay which represents the results of a specific traffic flow analysis over the network. Figure 8 represents a more sophisticated study of intercarrier traffic flow. All of these results may be displayed instantly on a large screen graphical terminal or be routed to a multicolour high resolution plotter.

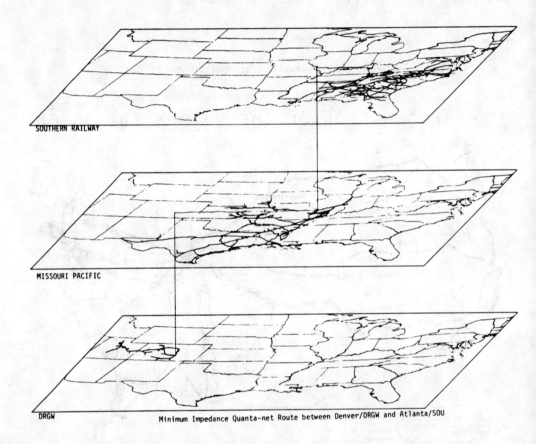

Fig. 8.   Analysis of inter-carrier traffic flow.

To put this study in the right perspective from the point of view of computation one should realize that the political map shown in Fig. 7 entails about 10,000 vectors and the network model includes about 18,000 nodes and about the same number of links. The transaction data base used may include anywhere between 1,000,000 and 100,000,000 bytes of information (it takes 1 byte to store an alphanumeric character, 4 bytes to store an integer number and 8 bytes to store a 'double precision' number). While the response of the system in the cases represented by Fig. 7 may be described as 'instant', the amount of analysis underlying Fig. 8 will depend of course on the complexity of the issues addressed, and typically it would take anywhere between a week and a month of work of the analytical team, which will consume between 1 to 10 hours of CPU time. In this process many figures of the kinds displayed by Figures 7 and 8 will be generated as intermediate results in the convergence process towards the final report.

Computer-aided Design

The next example, summarized in Figures 9-11, is taken from a design project for a discrete control network for a power system. The system may be reduced to a two-ports box with three sets of constraints for the input, output and power efficiency of the box. In the process of development of the design a computerized model has been used including anywhere between 20 to 100 coupled ordinary differential equations. The changing size of the computerized model reflected the evolving complexity of the design, which started with a classical 'text book' approach that did not work. The final design was represented by several hundreds of pages of graphical and tabular summaries of wave-forms of the various state variables of the system, under various case study conditions. The final design was then built as a prototype. This performed in excellent agreement with the computerized model.

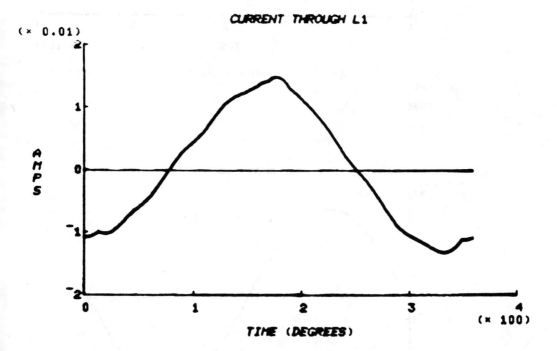

Fig. 9.   Modelling a discrete power control system: The voltage across a branch of the network.

This design took an extensive amount of computerized experimentation, which comprised numerous instant studies and instant results, which fed further ideas into the iterative solution process. The total study took several months with the accumulative CPU time estimated at 1 to 2 hours.

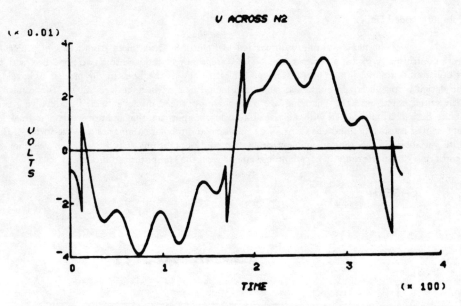

Fig. 10. Modelling a discrete power control system: The current through a branch of the network.

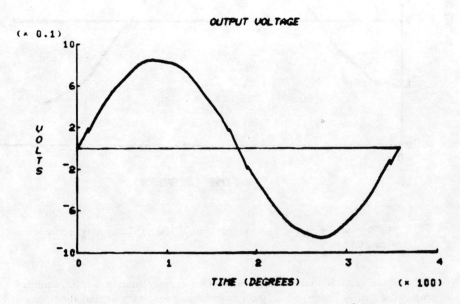

Fig. 11. Modelling a discrete power control system: output wave form.

COMPUTER SYSTEM CONSIDERATIONS

A key criterion to an interactive computer system is that its response to a trivial request from the keyboard will occur within a fraction of a second. This leaves open the definition of what is a trivial request. This statement may be turned around to state that a trivial request for an interactive system is anything it could respond to within a fraction of a second. The limiting factor would seem to be the amount of CPU time invoked by the interactive request. From this standpoint the illustrations represented by Figures 1-6 may be considered on our system as trivial requests. The fact that it takes longer in clock time to complete the response of the computer stems from two factors. One factor is the communication speed which comes into play because of the large volumes of data displayed on the graphical terminals (Tektronix 4013, 4015 and 4016). A more significant factor is due to the additional interaction between the user and the computer as called for by the application. It is not unusual for it to take about a minute to type a more sophisticated request, or as in the case of Fig. 6, several actions may be required. Here the completion of the response required 4 interactions, one when the program is invoked and the other three when the initial estimates are entered from the screen. It is interesting to note, however, that when the interaction is prolonged by the user's actions, this prolongation is not perceived by the user as an unacceptable delay.

The power of an interactive system may be measured by what is consiered as a trivial request. This is so because in the process of problem-solving, the trivial requests are leading towards the more sophisticated solutions. Thus, the more complicated the trivial requests are, the more powerful the tools invoked in the final analysis. If nonlinear regression (Fig. 6) is considered a trivial request then in most common applications the limits on the capabilities of the analyst are his or her imagination and/or a lack of the appropriate mathematical skills.

It is a commonly known syndrome of large centralized computer installations that at any given time a small number of users consume most of the resources of the machine. It is commonly argued also that one should split the user community into groups of small users and big users and let the big users justify a large machine while the small users be 'better' served by small machine(s). The thrust of the argument presented here indicates that I do not subscribe to this view but feel that this issue has to be addressed.

Inspection of the makeup of the large-user group makes it apparent that a typical big user is, most of the time, a small user while preparations are going on for the 'big run'. Similarly, inspection of the small-user group reveals that the nature of the applications developed is such that at least some of them will inevitably move to the big-user category. The capability to move back and forth between the two categories, without having to switch computers and systems, is extremely valuable in the problem solving environment. Any attempt at arbitrarily defining a dividing line between the two groups by assigning them to two separate computing environments results in the undesirable situation where the so called big user will continue to use the centralized system whether or not he may be categorized at the moment as a small or big user. More importantly, the user of the small machine dedicated to small applications will spend a tremendous amount of effort to fit his problem to his machine even when it developed to the point where it is better qualified as a 'big' application. We have experienced this phenomenon prior to acquiring our current system (August 79), where our user community was split between a large and powerful 'batch' machine (IBM/360/91) and a 'small' interactive system (IBM 370/158). In spite of the fact that the cycles of the big machine were priced at a much lower rate than those of the smaller one, the interactive machine reached saturation while the batch machine ran at about half capacity. Since the two were physically separate there was no way of shifting the unused resources of the one in order to augment the capacity of the other. The way it was eventually resolved was by replacing the two machines by one (IBM 3033) with enough capacity to serve both communities concurrently. As a matter of fact the system is being periodically tuned to shift resources to the continuously growing interactive side of the house from the steady 'batch side'.

LANGUAGE CONSIDERATIONS

Large centralized computer systems generally offer the user the advantage of all commonly-used computer languages. These facilities are needed in order to accommodate past investments in software packages which continue to serve their purposes. However, when discussing the development of interactive computer graphics facilities aimed at the future rather than the present computer environment one may have to be more selective. The following is a summary of the goals for our system:

1. Problem solving in Engineering and natural sciences.

2. Computing environment with hardly any technical support by computer specialists

3. One system to serve a user in the various stages of the solution process with no switching penalty when going from small to large applications and vice versa.

The prerequisite imposed on the future user of the system is in keeping with our emphasis on Engineering applications. Consequently, it is assumed that a user will be versed in the tools of applied mathematics commonly used by engineers, as well as in mathematical notation and syntax.

The lack of readily available technical help as well as the lack of aptitude of most engineering students for traditional computer programming, which they find painful and unrewarding, puts the onus on the designer of the computer system. He is compelled to dedicate a part of the power of the system to provide a more acceptable interface between the machine and the engineering user. A major step in this direction would be to integrate graphics into the interface in such a way as to eliminate most of the traditional voluminous input and output in the form of piles of printouts and punched cards. In just as important a step one would move to an interpreted language rather than a compiled one. For historical reasons traditional language requires of the user at least three steps:

1. Program creation: At this stage the user would either use the key punch or, in a more modern environment, he would use an on-line text editor to feed the computer with the text of a program.

2. Compilation: In this stage the user submits the program to the computer to check for internal consistency and convert it to a format used internally by the computer for execution. A good compiler will identify all the data-independent errors in the program, and

3. Execution: Often the execution stage comprises of several consecutive stages. However, it consists of at least one stage involving the user, who has to follow the prescribed procedure.

In contrast, in an interpreter-based language all these steps are lumped together and executed 'on the fly' when the user types a line on the computer terminal. As an example, consider the graphical illustration given above (Fig. 2) of the mathematical surface represented by $(\sin r) \div r$. To define the surface one has to define the field of r over which it is evaluated. Inspection of the figure reveals that the field of r is represented over a rectangular grid which is defined by 30 equal increments in both x and y directions. A set of equidistant points along an axis is encountered very often in graphics and programming in general. It may be easily defined in terms of the INDEX VECTOR which is a vector containing all integers between 1 and an arbitrary number, which in the above case would be 31. An engineer accustomed to greek symbols would not object to the use of the symbol ι as the index vector generator in the way that if N is an integer then ιN instructs the computer to create an index vector containing all integers between 1 and N. Thus

$$X \leftarrow \iota\, 5$$

would assign to the vector x the sequence 1 2 3 4 5. The vector x is created by the interpreter immediately after the user has typed the above line and pressed the RETURN key. Similarly

$$X \leftarrow (\imath 31) - 16$$

would instantly create a vector containing all integers between −15 and 15. One can define the y vector
over an identical range by assigning

$$Y \leftarrow X$$

Next, the field r is defined in terms of the conventional notation

$$r = (x^2 + y^2)^{1/2}$$

for all values of x and y in the ranges

$$- 15 \leqslant x, y \leqslant 15$$

This may be translated to the computer in terms of the discrete vectors x and y defined over the same
range. This translation should result into a rectangular (31 X 31) grid, where at each point the corresponding elements of x and y are squared, added and then the square root is evaluated. Denoting expo-
nentiation by *, one can define the field R in terms of a 31 X 31 matrix produced by the outer-sum
between x*2 and y*2, followed by the square root

$$R \leftarrow ((X*2) \circ . + Y*2) * 0.5$$

where the construct ° .+ denotes the outer sum to mean add each element of x*2 to all elements of y*2.
The outer sum operation is a special case of the more generalized function of the outer product. Now,
having defined the matrix R, one may invoke

$$TRIPLOT(SIN \ R) \div R$$

to obtain the illustration given in Fig. 2. The entire sequence of instructions may be summarized

$$X \leftarrow (\imath 31) - 16$$
$$R \leftarrow (A \circ . + A \leftarrow X*2) * 0.5$$
$$TRIPLOT \ (SIN \ R) \div R$$

as three instructions typed into the machine and executed instantly by the interpreter at the end of
entry of each line. If it is necessary to repeat this sequence often it may be encapsuled into a simple
USER DEFINED FUNCTION which contains the same sequence

```
      ∇ FIG2
[1]   X←(ı31)-16
[2]   R←(A°.+A←X*2)*0.5
[3]   TRIPLOT (SIN R)÷R
      ∇
```

which is saved and will always produce Fig. 2 upon typing FIG2.

The above example is not intended as a tutorial to the language used for these applications, which is beyond the scope of the present chapter. It is intended as a demonstration to the mathematically oriented user of the level of the power, flexibility, conciseness and simplicity at which a computer may be approached in a problem solving environment. Furthermore, attention is drawn to the simple fashion at which basic graphics are integrated into the system. A more detailed expose of the syntax of the language would lead to programming constructs like

$$PLOT \ Y \ MINUS \ INTEG \ 1 \ DERIV \ (Y \leftarrow EXP - X*2) VS \ X \leftarrow 0.1 \times (\iota 101) - 51$$

which may be typed directly to produce Fig. 1 as shown above.

DISCUSSION

There are two somewhat controversial issues underlying this presentation. The first one has to do with the choice of the centralized mainframe computer as the vehicle for the development of our interactive system. This choice, which was made in 1974, has resulted in a viable powerful system which today carries the bulk of our educational and new research activities in the school. It is the growing momentum behind the interactive system which played the major role in the decision to expand our capabilities by moving to the use of a machine of the capacity of an IBM 3033 computer. At peak load time we see close to 100 interactive users on the system representing a load similar to that of the batch activity which together utilize about 60% of the available resources of the computer. We expect the interactive load to reach above the level of 200 simultaneous users before impacting the performance of the system. This balance between the number of simultaneous interactive users and the capacity of the computer is very valuable to the user since he can obtain a burst of computer power as frequently or infrequently as his application calls for without having to justify and maintain his own computer.

The second issue which is still quite controversial is the choice of language for the development of interactive computer graphics as a general purpose problem solving tool. Although all common computer languages are available on the system, the language chosen for the local development and promotion of interactive computer graphics is APL, which is to date the major language used in the interactive side of the system. In retrospect it is considered as a most rewarding choice which has led to the fast development of a viable and efficient system, as well as a supportive body of students, faculty and administrators. A detailed description of APL is beyond the scope of the present chapter, however, it is hoped that the reader was exposed to the power and flavour of the highly mathematical language through the examples given above.

A third key element behind the power of our system is the VM/370 operating system which manages the hardware of the computer. The operating system provides each user with his own virtual machine with a very high degree of independence from the other users on the system and also with a high degree of independence within the actual physical resources available. Of particular importance is the capability of the user to change, from the terminal, the size of his virtual computer to up to 16 million bytes, without changing his application software or anything else.

In summary, it is a combination of three elements which makes our system powerful for interactive problem solving: the simplicity and flexibility of APL-Graphics, a flexible workspace size as offered by VM370, and the availability of a tremendous computer power in burst mode, as provided by the IBM 3033 computer.

REFERENCES

1. Y. Hazony, Computers & Graphics, 2, 209-218 (1977).
2. Y. Hazony, Computers & Graphics, 4, 165-176 (1979).
3. Y. Hazony, Computers & Graphics, 4, 63-75 (1979).

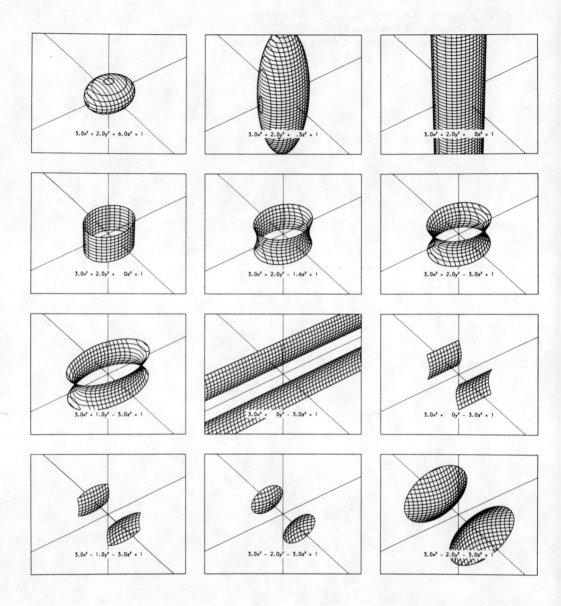

These are some of the 'quadric surfaces' that can be formed from the general equation $ax^2 + by^2 + cz^2 = d$. They are three-dimensional surfaces that can be used to 'patch' an object (see page 26). Such surfaces have many useful properties and this family was drawn for the Open University Mathematics Course M203, Topics in Pure Mathematics, programme 16, **Quadric Surfaces**.

COMBINING COMPUTER ANIMATION AND TELEVISION PRESENTATION :

A CASE STUDY – THE OPEN UNIVERSITY MATHEMATICS COURSE

John C. Gilbert   Graphics Section, University of London Computer Centre

John Richmond   BBC – Open University Production Centre

The techniques of television presentation are well established and efficient for conveying educational information. If computer animation can be successfully integrated into conventional production schedules, it can open up new fields of educational experience. This chapter gives an account of a collaboration that has proved very successful. A number of interesting lessons have been learnt about the requirements for successful integrated and the design and construction of images.

The Open University is a multi-media distance teaching organisation. One part of its manifold is the Television Programme. Over the years a particular strategy has evolved for the teaching of mathematics that makes good use of all the media; within the television programmes, one tactic that has proved successful is the computer generation of graphic images. This chapter explores the factors that influence this success.

To appreciate the role that computer animation plays, it is important to understand its context and the way in which the Open University deploys its various media. We shall confine outselves to the Mathematics Foundation Course (M101). This course starts at approximately 'O' level standard (USA grade 12), includes much of the basic calculus teaching at 'A' level (Freshman level) and progresses beyond that into other areas to provide a good foundation for future studies.

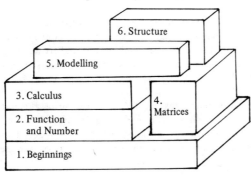

The Block Structure of M101 (Each block = 5 units)

The M101 course is spread over 32 study weeks with a requirement of 10 hours study each week. The backbone of the week's work is a printed course text — a teaching text with narrative, diagrams, exercises and self-assessment questions. Each of these texts is divided into sections representing some 90 minutes to 2 hours work. One of these sections is based upon a 25 minute television programme (transmitted during the study week), while another is based upon a 20 minute section of audio tape mailed to the student with the correspondence material. The division of a typical course text may be shown thus:

1. Introduction and initial reading section.

2. Narrative — developing new ideas with many diagrams and examples.

3. Television section   3.1 Pre-programme work
                         3.2 Programme Summary — key points
                                              — diagrams
                         3.3 Post programme work and follow-up material.

4. Tape section — the tutor on the tape guides the student through diagrams
                 and examples.

5. Narrative — further reading and consolidation.

6. Conclusions and recapitulation.

For what purpose then, is television used? The best answer is that television is used to provide students with information that they could not get in any other way. Graphics and models are employed to capture the essence of the mathematics and to convey the spirit of the main ideas. The television programmes are not considered to be televised lectures. The aim is to use the power of the medium and its associated technologies to present the most interesting and intriguing aspects of the mathematics in as inviting, warm engaging a fashion as possible. By producing 25 minutes of television that our students will find absorbing we can not only help them with difficult ideas, but we can also bring the mathematics alive and make it more fun.

It is here that the computer animation comes in. The accuracy of a graph drawn by computer is more immediately convincing than that of one drawn by hand. The precision of the microfilm recorder transfers to the television screen and is accepted by the viewers. Conventional graphics animators are highly skilled and can draw diagrams or curves with considerable accuracy; there is in computer animation, however, a precision of line and a smoothness of movement that manages to project the essence of the mathematics itself.

At a recent conference of the British Universities Film Council on computer animation we were able to demonstrate how we deploy computer animations to convey images that cannot be conveyed by text alone. Yet in this article we are confined to text and so we find ourselves in a 'Catch 22' predicament: trying to use the printed page alone; we therefore must rely a good deal on your imagination.

Students see conventional graphics (text or TV) as representing the mathematics they are studying, they see computer generated graphics as the real thing; in effect, they see actual mathematics happening before their very eyes. The demonstration of mathematics in action, compared with the traditional use of static diagrams, is one of the more important aspects of our use of computer animations.

For example in one programme we wanted to depict the nature of quadratic and cubic mathematical functions.

The graph of the quadratic function $ax^2 + bx + c$ is a parabola:

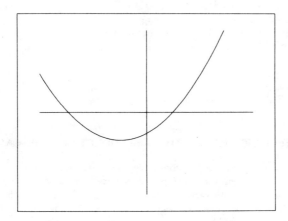

but the nature of the whole 'family of parabolas' is not fully realised until the different parabolas, arising from different values of the parameters a, b and c, have been explored. We could present four different parabolas:

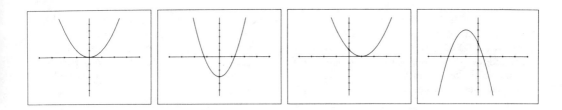

but here the diagrams are so static. Computer animation enables us to vary a, b and c independently and see how the shape of the curve changes. The provision of an image which shows all the intermediate stages is important to students. It enables them to grasp the idea that there is an infinite number of parabolas; short, fat, high, low, tall and wide (and all between, as well). Because an animation can be obtained by simply changing one coefficient, say 'a', in the function, and so make the parabolas 'flap its wings', we show that the general quadratic is not a set of separate curves but one flexible curve which flexes in a certain characteristic way. In observing this, our students will see, for example, that one special case of a parabola is a straight line which occurs at the instant the curvature of the parabola changes from curving up to curving down:

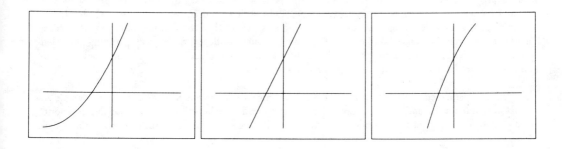

Now, a student's first encounter with the parabola is not the occasion to make the point that a straight line is a special (degenerate) case of a parabola. In fact, it can be counter-productive to burden the student with such detail. However, the computer animation makes that point easily, without fuss, and at an intuitive level without going through a formal exposition. Given the viewers' acceptance of the computer's innate honesty, we can strike the right academic balance. Nevertheless, it is probably these extra ideas, which are implicit in a complete animation, which make the computed images fascinating.

Many observers remark that this kind of exploration in mathematics leads to higher levels of understanding while conveying not only the excitement but also the beauty of mathematics.

THE TELEVISION PROGRAMME – PRODUCTION TIMESCALES

The education potential for computer animation is enormous, but it is important to appreciate that the computer graphics for the Open University have to be commissioned and produced in a very short time-scale, which can vary between 2 months and 2 weeks. The annual requirement may be for as many as 15 to 20 sequences, ranging from 30 seconds to 3 minuntes. But at the beginning of the year it is almost impossible to predict the pattern of demand beyond rather broad possibilites.

The television images discussed in this chapter arrive at the Open University Studios as 16mm film. This film must be complete as planned before it can be run into the programme. For this to be the case, the animations must be accurately commissioned.

The real problem in commissioning computer animation is the same as for any other television resource. It arises from the production schedule – work cannot start until the content of course texts has been settled. But the work must be **finished** before the course units are sent to the course editor, who ensures that text and television programme correlate correctly. In particular, diagrams in the text cannot be finally agreed before the television programme is recorded in case last minute changes are made.

The design process for computer graphics is an interactive one. If we are to take full advantage of the creative ideas that emerge in devising programmes, the print schedule must allow for the final editing of course units to be done **after** the completion of the corresponding programme. This is not possible in the Open University. The University runs its courses from February to October each year. For each course there must be scheduled mailings if students are to receive the printed material in time (particularly to enable briefing ahead of scheduled broadcasts) and time must be allowed for materials to be printed, proof read, reprinted, packaged and warehoused. Final editing dates, then, are fixed by counting backwards from the mailing date, rather than by the needs of animation designers.

At the beginning, it is always possible to devise an orderly schedule of overlapping productions, but, taking account of the availability of people and resources, and allowing for accidents and emergencies, the actual progress will be fairly chaotic. It requires about three months to make a programme. The first month is taken up by a working group of academics, producers and consultants mulling over ideas and considering possibilities. The end of the second month should see the final programme design agreed, and it is during this period that the commissioning of materials, including computer animations, begins. The third month is devoted to final planning, detailed scripting, and rehearsals, culminating in the studio day. One producer will be running several programmes in parallel, each at a different stage related to its particular transmission date.

Since the commissioning of computer graphics has to be precise, it is rarely possible to specify any animation until it is certain that the script will not be subject to further development. Ideally, detailed specifications should be made about six weeks before the studio date. Usually it is less, and on a few occasions it has been as little as two weeks prior to the recording. Accordingly, we have to be pragmatic in the way we use computer animation and we need a clear, precise method of commissioning. In the following sections we will address first the problem of design and use of computer animation before dealing with these methods of commissioning.

COMPUTER ANIMATION – HARNESSING ITS EDUCATIONAL POTENTIAL

The producer's first task is to assemble a group of people to form an ideas 'think tank' to consider how to use the medium of television most effectively. Computer animation is not exempt from the battle between the academic's desire to get the facts right and the producer's need to create something which will leave a real impression on the student. Television is, or should be, a dynamic medium, and it offers many devices to the tutor that are unrealisable in traditional classroom teaching. A good example is the provision of movement by computer animation. Feed-back from students consistently picks out computer animation, with its dynamic quality, as one key element in the television programmes. Although movement is compulsive in its own right, we must ensure that the images created genuinely advance our students' mathematical perceptions.

In mathematics, once you have come to understand something, it can be very difficult to look back and see where it was that you failed to grasp the point. In fact, at the moment of perception even highly intelligent people will often chastise themselves for their earlier obtuseness. Those with experience in mathematics education will appreciate that students' ideas develop slowly. Students frequently need a variety of demonstrations and illustrations to couple with their own experience before they can begin to understand a specific piece of mathematics. Computer graphics provides just one tool, albeit an efficient one for the production of these demonstrations.

Our problem as producers and designers, is to capture the compulsive nature of the moving graphic and, at the same time, to tell a story that will intrigue, but remain within the framework of 'teaching' mathematics. Simplicity is important, not just because there are only a few weeks in which to produce each animation, but because it is necessary to give the students a chance to perceive things for themselves. The simpler the image, the more likely they are to get the point. We shall discuss later some of the lessons we have learned which are relevant to the process of devising animations; first, however, we will describe some animations in their context.

In designing animations we have to consider three levels at which our students will respond to the images provided.

1. Pictorial level – The fascinating and compulsive nature of the image and
   its movement.

2. Teaching level – The direct illustration of the teaching points made.

3. Intuitive level – The presentation of 'hidden meanings'; leading the student
   to an appreciation of side-issues or special cases that may
   not be specifically taught.

A topic which illustrates these aspects is **Complex Numbers**. (For non-mathematicians this is to do with a new kind of number, the square root of -1.) In the following 3 pages we describe how we used computer animation to capture a particular concept. Once again we face the problem of describing a dynamic image using only words and static diagrams. It will take you some time to read through these pages yet the sequences took only 3 minutes of screen time. However we do hope you will be able to get some feel for what we were trying to achieve. These 'complex' numbers occur, for example, in the general solution of quadratic equations; this was the story we wished to tell.

The solutions of the equations $x^2 - 4x + 3 = 0$ are, in graphical terms, the points where the graph of $y = x^2 - 4x + 3$ cuts the x-axis. In the diagram you can see that these are $x = 1$ and $x = 3$.

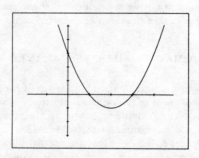

The question is, what happens when we change the equation slightly by changing the last figure, 3, into say 5. Will the new equation $x^2 - 4x + 5 = 0$ have a solution? The corresponding graph of the new function has exactly the same **shape** as before but, with a 5 instead of a 3, it is placed 2 units higher.

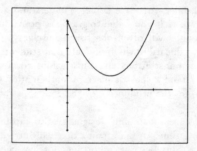

Now you see **no** intersections and so the equations has no solutions. Is that not a little unfair? Why should $x^2 - 4x + 3 = 0$ have solutions yet $x^2 - 4x + 5 = 0$ have none? The dilemma is reinforced when we realise that the quadratic formula will give a solution to both equations, but for $x^2 - 4x + 5 = 0$ it involves the square root of -1. The solutions are $2 \pm \sqrt{-1}$. These numbers, called complex numbers, differ from the numbers to which we are accustomed. It is usual to represent ordinary numbers, 'real' numbers, as being strung out horizontally along a 'number' line:

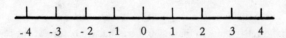

For 'complex' numbers a vertical direction is added to cope with multiples of $\sqrt{-1}$. Each complex number is then represented by a point in the plane:

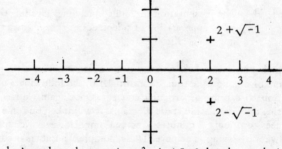

So with the new 'complex' numbers the equation $x^2 - 4x + 5 = 0$ **does** have solutions after all.

To link the two cases together into a coherent story we developed the following animation for the television programme which introduced complex numbers.

Stage 1.

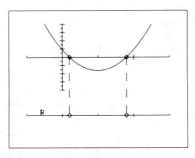

This is a quadratic where the graph does cut the x-axis. You can see the solutions were plotted on the number line, directly below the graph.

Stage 2. The graph was moved upwards (as the equation changed) and the solutions moved closer to each other until they met (frame 2). The graph continued upwards.

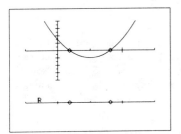 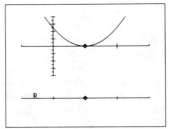 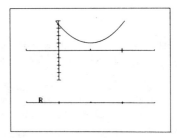

As the graph moves higher, there is no intersection and the solutions disappear. The question remains — how can the two points, moving towards each other, suddenly disappear? Where did they go?

As the graph moved up and down crossing and leaving the x-axis, the points on the lower line were seen to approach each other, make contact and vanish — only to reappear again as soon as the graph came down.

The movement, appearance and disappearance of the two points was visually intriguing. It posed the intuitive idea that the points should not disappear and that somehow the story had to have a happy ending. This paved the way for the introduction of 'complex' numbers and the next animation revealed all.

Stage 3. The solutions were now plotted on the complex number diagram rather than the simple number line.

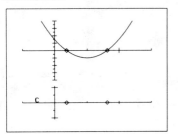 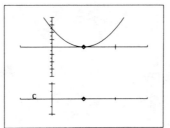 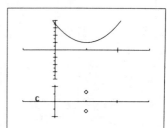

As before, the solution points were seen to move along the 'real' axis until they met each other, but this time, instead of disappearing, they just separated, moving in a vertical direction; moving off the 'real' number line into the 'complex' plane. So, with the new mathematical concept of complex number, the solutions do not disappear at all but move about the plane. Resolving the mystery sets off a chain reaction of curiosity. If the quadratic equation can behave in this new way, what about the other equations? This question led to the next stage:

Stage 4. The visual exploration was repeated for a cubic equation (beginning with x^3) and the movement of its solutions was plotted in the same way corresponding to changes in the cubic curve.

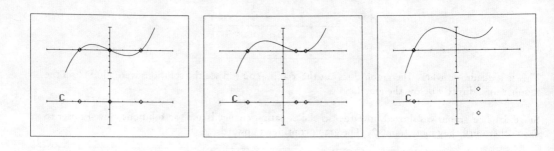

The animation first showed the three 'real' solutions. As the curve moved up, the right hand pair approached each other. Having met, they separated. But there are still three solutions. As the curve went down, the left hand pair approached each other, coalesced, and split vertically. Still three solutions. Animating the cubic curve through all its possible shapes was gripping enough, but watching how the solutions moved in concert with the curve was quite amazing. Even mathematicians and experienced teachers found the experience unique and stimulating.

There are several hidden messages in this animation sequence. One was that complex solutions **always** occur in pairs, being reflections of each other in the horizontal (real) axis. Although we did not make specific reference to this point in the commentary, the image is there and our students will have observed it. Certainly the image was ripe for the mathematical analysis later in the course. At this stage in the television programme, interest was running high and to capitalise on this we conducted a final computer exploration. We looked at the solutions of a quartic equation. The quartic (beginning with x^4) is seen to have 4 solutions. These behave in a similar way — pairs approaching each other, coalescing, and splitting up in a vertical direction; when paired off this way they are seen to move about the complex plane always in pairs, just as if the x-axis were a mirror.

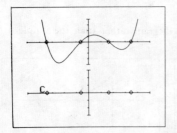 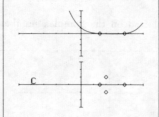 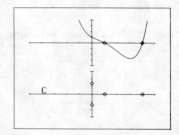

Now this animation reveals another intuitive idea. This quartic or **fourth** degree equation has **four** roots; what about a fifth degree equation? The intuitive answer of five is correct. In fact the progression from 2nd, 3rd and 4th degree equations paved the way for a more generalised study later in the course. Although the animation was simple, from the educational point of view it was extremely effective.

Another example of the use of computer animations to tell a story came in the calculus section of M101, with a topic entitled **Taylor Approximations**. (For the non-mathematician, this is the branch of mathematics which enables an electronic calculator to work out the sine of an angle. Memories of school tell you that you have to draw a right-angled triangle and calculate the ratio of OPPOSITE and HYPOTENUSE. Clearly the calculator does not draw triangles, nor were sines in 'log tables' calculated this way). The question is, how can you calculate a sine without drawing triangles? This was the essence of the story to be told by the television programme. As calculators can only work out formulae which involve the operations $+, -, \times, \div$ the television programme set out to illustrate the formula which gives a good approximation to sin(x). This formula, called the Taylor Approximation, is

$$x - \frac{x^3}{3!} + \frac{x^5}{5!} - \dots \qquad\qquad \dots \text{ and so on using}$$

as many terms as necessary to give an accurate answer. Although it looks fearsome, a calculator is able to cope with this formula by calculating a sequence of values

first x

then $x - \dfrac{x^3}{3 \times 2 \times 1}$

then $x - \dfrac{x^3}{3 \times 2 \times 1} + \dfrac{x^5}{5 \times 4 \times 3 \times 2 \times 1}$

and proceeding to add the next term from the formula until the value described is effectively unchanged by the addition of further terms. The theory, which involved calculus, provides the mathematical reasons why it works. But logical proof is often a long way from an intuitive understanding. We use computer animation to provide students with visual evidence and so help them to acquire a 'belief' that the theory works. Essentially, the demonstrations were to show that the sine, whose graph oscillates forever, could be represented by a combination of powers of x whose graphs do not oscillate at all. The television animations were designed to show the approximation graphically, and to show how it improved as successive terms were added.

In this way, our students were able to make their own judgement of the approximation. Indeed, active audience participation was invited by asking students to see how many terms were required to give a good approximation over a whole cycle.

The following illustrations show various stages in the animation.

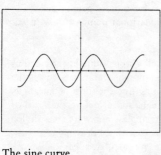

The sine curve.

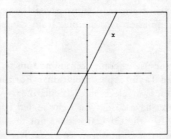

Here is x, the first
approximation

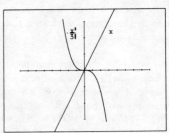

now the x^3 term

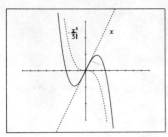

add, and you get

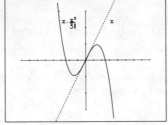

the second approximation

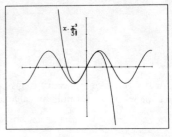

Compare with the sine curve—

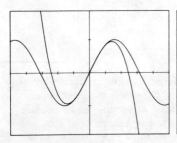

zoom in to see how
close they are.

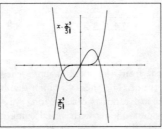

Introduce the x^5
term

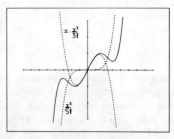

add, to give

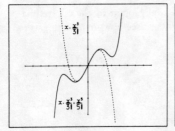

the next approximation.

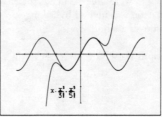

Compare with the sine curve

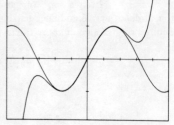

zoom in to examine the wiggles.

Now an experiment. The arrows show the difference between the sine curve and the approximation, which is of degree 7 — note the term in x^7.

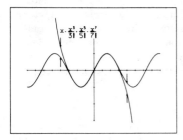

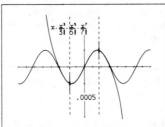

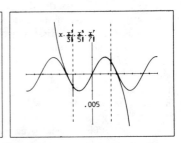

Introduce arrows

the number shows the difference as they move outwards for degree 7.

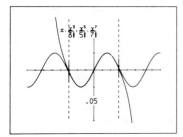

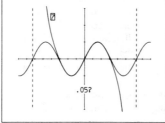

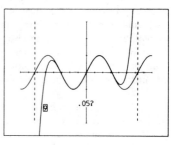

It is 0.05 for one cycle.
(Visually, where the
curves seem to separate)

Which approximation will give
0.05 for two cycles ?

9th degree

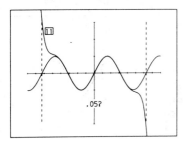

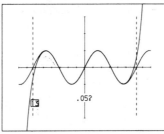

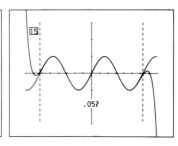

11th degree

13th degree — nearly there

15th degree

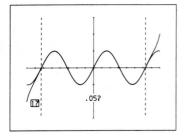

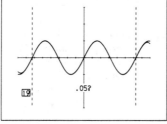

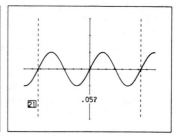

17th degree— looks OK

19th wiggles all the way

21st cannot tell the difference

THE COMPUTER ANIMATION — COMMISSIONING

Whereas the design and utilisation of computer animation is the producer's responsibility, the translation of these ideas to an actual image on film is the domain of the graphics computer programmer. The commissioning phase is the interface between these two. The success of the completed animation is usually a direct reflection of the care and attention paid in commissioning. The outcome of the commissioning must be a detailed specification — most probably a storyboard — from which the animator can work. By ensuring an interactive relationship between producer and programmer we are able to use the computer facilities to best effect, especially when the animation is required, in final form, in a few weeks.

The normal situation would be for early contact between the producer and programmer to discuss possible requirements and to ascertain their practicality. Certain ideas may be rejected through budgetary constraints or limitations in available time. This early meeting also enables the animator to suggest ways in which the medium can be used most effectively to deal with the particular topic. The producer will also be seeking to learn what freedom of movement is available in relation to the basic sequence he has in mind, and how he may best highlight significant features. The programmer will be more interested in the nature of the computational exercise that will be necessary; he will, after all, be entering into a commitment to complete the work to schedule. Occasionally it has been found helpful to produce 35mm still frames of possible stages in the animation, in order that both parties can visualize a complicated mathematical function and determine the best method of demonstrating the principal theme, utilising the screen area in an efficient and sensible manner.

The producer next prepares a detailed storyboard in consultation with other members of the course team. A second meeting will then be held and any outstanding problems resolved. The producer will run through the storyboard and write the full version of the commentary which has been at the back of his mind for some time. In this way, detailed timings and final revisions will be made. This finalising stage is crucial, as subsequent changes to the specification could prove expensive, both in computing resources and software effort. Anticipation of potential variations is most important. Should the producer have any suspicion that there may be late changes in layout, or that zooms or pans may be requested later, then indication of such likelihood at this stage can enable them to be accommodated in the programming phase. This can be of immense value where two (or more) related and similar sequences are required but may not be commissioned together.

From the programming viewpoint, the concern is less with the complexity of the mathematics and more with the complexity of movement, particularly if there are several independent movements. Consideration of these factors enables the programmer to indicate whether the studio deadline can be met. In order to give a little more flexibility it has become increasingly common for a basic storyboard to be prepared without all of its timings set. Provided the layout and actions are fixed, programming can begin with the timings as variables which can be specified at a later stage.

The following storyboard indicates the detail required. There would normally be, in addition, a carefully drafted layout of the screen area giving the required positioning and relative scaling of text, axes etc. A composite is generally adequate; this will show all the relevant features derived from various key-frames.

In this instance, the programmer (JCG) has a mathematical background, and so the producer (JR) may assume that the mathematical terminology is understood. This in turn enables us to work with fairly brief but accurate technical specifications. The storyboard needs to be sufficiently detailed to enable the programmer to generate the whole sequence — all movements and associated changes must be carefully specified.

Storyboard for M101/14 Sequence 3

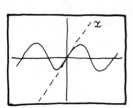

Hold 10 secs

Curves $y = x$, $y = \sin x$

Caption x $[y = x$ dashed$]$

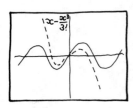

In 1 sec
(simultaneously)....Fade out $y = x$ curve and caption x

Fade in $y = x - \frac{x^3}{3!}$ curve (dashed)

and $x = \frac{x^3}{3!}$ caption

Hold $\boxed{A}$ secs

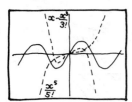

Jump on caption $\frac{x^5}{5!}$ and dashed curve

Hold $\boxed{B}$ secs

In 1 sec ....Fade off captions $x - \frac{x^3}{3!}$ and $\frac{x^5}{5!}$

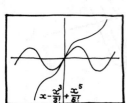

In 4 secs..........Run in curve $y = \frac{x^3}{3!} + \frac{x^5}{5!}$

and wipe off dashed curves at same time
(at same x)
Jump on caption $x - \frac{x^3}{3!} + \frac{x^5}{5!}$

Hold $\boxed{C}$ secs
In 1 sec ....Fade off sine curve
Hold $\boxed{D}$ secs

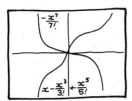

Jump on caption $-\frac{x^7}{7!}$

Hold $\boxed{E}$ secs

In $\boxed{F}$ secs........Run in curve $y = \frac{-x^7}{7!}$

Hold $\boxed{G}$ secs

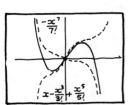

In $\boxed{H}$ secs ....Run in curve $x - \frac{x^3}{3!} + \frac{x^5}{5!} - \frac{x^7}{7!}$

wiping previous curves to dashes
(at same x)

Hold $\boxed{I}$ secs

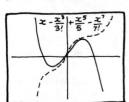

In 1 sec ....Fade out $y = \frac{-x^7}{7!}$ curve and caption

and caption (only) $x - \frac{x^3}{3!} + \frac{x^5}{5!}$

Hold $\boxed{J}$ secs

Jump on caption $x - \frac{x^3}{3!} + \frac{x^5}{5!} + \frac{x^7}{7!}$

Hold $\boxed{K}$ secs

The following example of the commissioning process illustrates the appropriate inter-action between producer and programmer. In this instance the first contact was by telephone to enquire about the possibility of a short sequence to be used in connection with catastrophe theory. The primary aim was to explore the surface described by $y = -x^3 - ax$ in the range -1 to $+1$ for each of the variables x, y and a. This surface is shown here, as sketched by the producer:

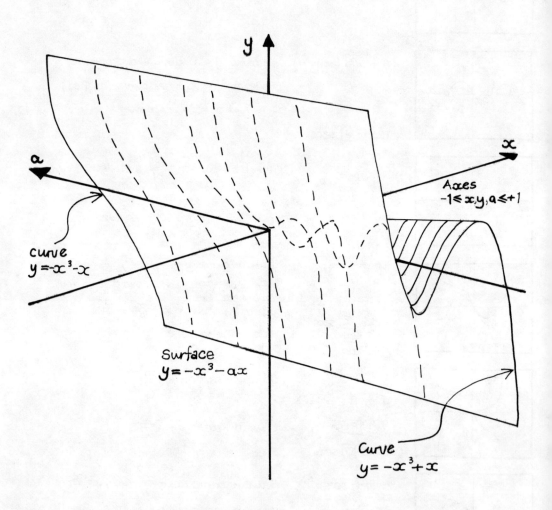

The first step was the production of still frames from a number of viewpoints and with different spacings of the individual curves.

The rough script was developed for discussion purposes. After several meetings bet-ween the producer and course team, a further meeting was arranged. For pedagogical reasons it had now been decided that a rotation of the surface should be made and a new (though similar) surface definition applied. A complete —and final— storyboard could now be drawn (with timings omitted).

Extract from Storyboard M101/14 Sequence 2

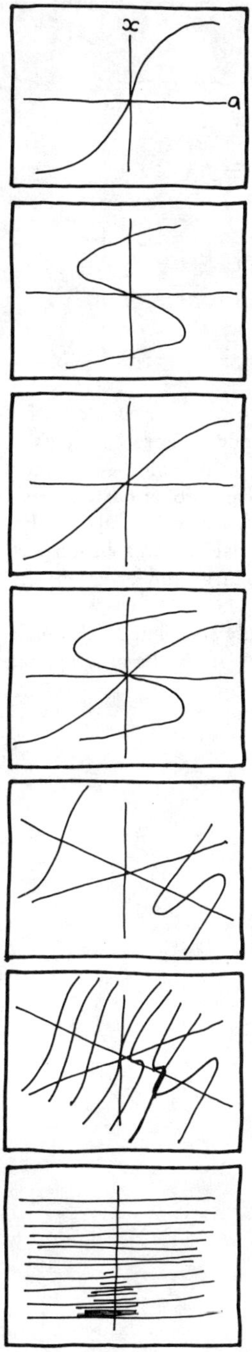

$$a = -x^3 - bx$$

Hold axes 5 secs *NO PERSPECTIVE

In 4 secs.......... Draw on curve $b = 0$ (bottom left to top right)

Hold 2 secs

Jump off

Hold 1 sec

In 4 secs......... Draw on curve $b = +1$

Hold 2 secs

Jump off

Hold 1 sec

In 4 secs.......... Draw on curve $b = -1$

Hold 4 secs

In 6 secs......... Continuously vary b from -1 to $+1$

Hold 2 secs

In 6 secs......... then back to -1, but retain curve $b = -1$

Hold 2 secs

In 5 secs......... Rotate (view from $x = 1$ $a = -2$ $b = 2$)

Hold 1 sec   *With simultaneous increase in perspective
                from zero to full

In 5 secs........... Fill in surface, back edge to front —
                with leading bright curve

Hold 10 secs

In 8 secs.......... Rotate (view from +ve x axis)

Hold 10 secs

The changes in the storyboard (marked*) were made at the final meeting between producer and programmer during which a major problem was discussed at length and finally resolved. The problem
concerned the final image of the surface. This was to be from a view along the positive x-axis.

Clearly, to show the fold in the surface, a perspective projection is required. (The following frame shows the final surface projected with no perspective; this may be compared with the last frame of the actual sequence).

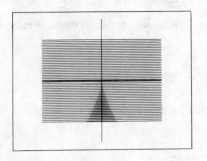 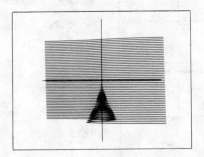

However, from the first part of the storyboard, it will be seen that the view along the b-axis is required and this should reveal cubic curves with no impression of depth. For these curves (excepting $b = 0$) a perspective view would distort the function and (importantly) stills from the sequence would not show the true cubic. This dilemma was resolved by introducing a proportional change from no perspective to full perspective during the initial rotation of the curves. Should this device fail visually, so forcing a rethink, it was decided to make the computer program readily emendable. This solution was made possible through the interactive nature of the relationship between producer and programmer.

When the final timings were supplied the animation was successfully completed. Although a relatively simple sequence with few movements, it proved very effective in its place in the programme.

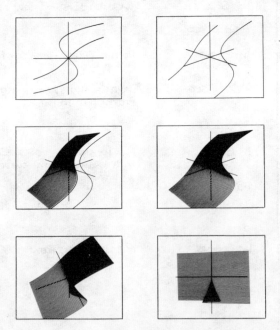

If they have an open-minded approach to the commissioning, both producer and programmer contribute to the successful animation. The producer may impart the basic visual presentation while the programmer will interject his experience of various techniques related to computer graphics. This pooling of knowledge has been a major factor in the fruitful collaboration we report here.

THE COMPUTER ANIMATION – GENERATION

It is beyond the scope of this chapter to go into detail about software techniques. These techniques enable the producer's storyboard to be interpreted in a manner suitable for computer processing to give the film sequence as the resultant output. As a first step the storyboard is analysed to isolate critical aspects of the sequence. Then any existing utilities must be located (for instance, to access a library of mathematical computer programs to perform required mathematical calculations). New (program) modules are written to provide the facilities not already catered for. All these items must be drawn together and controlled by a driving program which will initiate the construction (or drawing) of each individual frame. The driving program will also schedule the transitions between frames to accord with the specified timings. The number of **new** frames each second need not be the same for all movements.

The computer generated animations that are the subject of this chapter have all originated from one system. This is the one at the University of London Computer Centre. Powerful linked computers, Control Data 7600, 6600 and 6400, are used to process the computer programs. These have interfaced directly with DIMFILM (Descriptive Instructions for MicroFILM), a software package to produce the necessary instructions for the off-line plotting system. The film is exposed in a CalComp 1670 microfilm recorder, which produces high resolution images on perforated 16mm (or, for 'still' purposes, unperforated 35mm) reversal film via a precision cathode ray tube (CRT). The exposed film is reversal processed (in-house) to yield a clear white image on a dense black background. The device is a vector plotter, and, as such, is primarily suited to monochrome line drawings. Plotting speed is extremely fast, and, coupled with the power of the computer mainframes, complex animations can be produced in a reasonable time scale. A typical two minute sequence may require 20 seconds of 7600 central processor time and occupy the plotter for, perhaps, 20 minutes. With local film processing, the finished product is normally available within 24 hours of submitting the computer program.

The generation process is iterative in that several runs may be needed to produce a program that is correct in syntax and logic, and to ensure that every detail of the completed sequence is as required. It is particularly important to ensure that transitions within the animation are consistent and that movements of independent segments of the picture are uniformly maintained.

In the computer programming there is a need to balance flexibility with efficiency. Flexibility offers the producer the ability to make late changes to the script, but it may entail considerable effort by the programmer – possibly expensive effort if the facility is subsequently unused. It is a simple matter to accommodate variable timings. However, if the producer wants a split screen with an independent zoom for either part, the logical construction of the computer program would be quite distinct from that for a single static view. If the possibility of such a change has been envisaged at the commissioning stage the sequence could be programmed to permit a simple change introducing the new feature. For unforeseen major changes it may be debatable whether it is more economical to emend the existing computer program or start the whole program anew.

There is a good case for making all timings variable; it is often necessary to make small adjustments to the duration of movements and holds, so that the final pace at which the animation progresses can be finely tuned to the rest of the programme. There is however an accompanying danger that such facilities will creep into misuse and allow expensive experimentation to replace the design process. This is particularly true if variability is extended to pictorial composition.

In conventional film animation the final, detailed, storyboard embodies design decisions and, once film has been shot and the money has been spent, the producer and animator must live with the result. Apart from a line or colour test, there is not much room for playing with the animation medium. The design process must be one of applied skill and experience with repeated re-appraisal before the production stage.

The present system offered by the computer animator is flexible in that it allows for variations in production runs, provided they are within the same overall design.

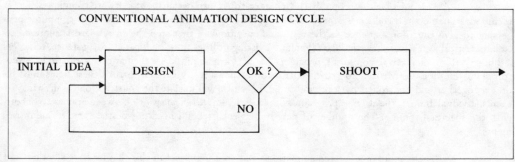

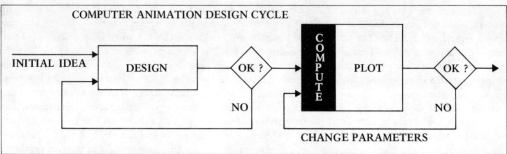

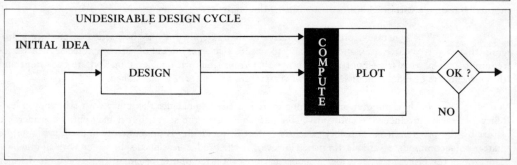

Although there are benefits of such flexibility, there are hidden dangers. Great flexibility presents a way for programme makers to launch into production without fully thinking through the design process. With advanced technology the design/production loop could become merged. In our view it would be regrettable if the flexibility of the system tempted people into design by trial and error instead of through interactions in which ideas get thrown around between producer and animator. In commissioning conventional animation there is a prerequisite: fully to understand the visual medium and to keep the design process tight with constant reappraisal during the design and commissioning stages before initiating the final production. It would be sad to lose the positive aspects of that sort of professionalism because we are entering the era of interactive design.

REFLECTIONS – LESSONS LEARNED

Even with simple animations it is easy to convey the wrong impression. We have learned the hard way and have made some 'classic' mistakes. Fortunately most have been correctable at a late stage (a positive attribute of flexibility). For example, in one animation we wished to show the effect of changing the constant 'c' in the formula $y = mx + c$, which defines a straight line. This change simply moves each point of the straight line graph in a vertical direction.

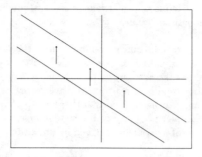

As any mathematician will tell you the straight line in question is infinite and therefore, must be seen to be infinite, i.e. to go off the screen. So it is not unreasonable for the academics to want the television screen to look like:

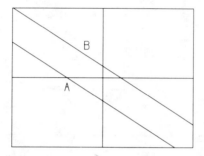

Unfortunately the transition from position A to position B is perceived by the eye as a diagonal movement. With no identifiable reference points on the line, the brain interprets the move as a displacement at right angles to the line itself – this being the minimum displacement.

Had the picture been designed differently, showing a line of finite length, the movement from A to B would be seen as vertical. This is because the eye would have the end points of the line for reference.

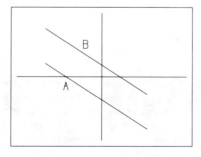

Most of the difficulties or mistakes arise from the poor composition of the picture which will be presented as a dynamic image. Being mathematicians, the production team will be clear in their own minds what interpretation should be made of each animation. Because the students are new to many of the ideas, difficulties may arise that are difficult to anticipate. Each time we design an animation we must try to be aware of this kind of problem. The students will see the animation for the first time during the programme; they have to assimilate the overall design, observe changes, digest implications and draw conclusions. Commentary alone is insufficient to direct students in this learning process; all key issues must be identified and emphasised visually.

      In considering the screen layout, we enquire where the viewer's eye will be focussed. With a static image, the layout helps us to make judgements on where the eye should dwell. However, when the picture is changing, we have to take account of the way movements attract the eye. If the commentary directs the viewer to specific visual information, we have to make judgements on how long it will take the eye and brain to respond, bearing in mind that there will perhaps be some other movement that competes for attention. For example, we produced a histogram representing a statistical probability distribution for the particular value of a variable displayed in a box (here .350).

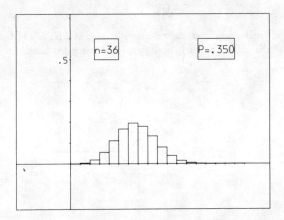

In the static picture given here the eye is free to scan the shape of the histogram and then examine the quantity in the box at the right. As this number increases the 'peak' of the histogram moves from left to right. The reader can examine this at his leisure from the series of plots shown.

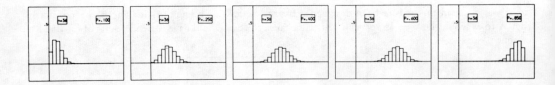

      The printed medium permits the reader to concentrate attention as required; you are free to scan the sequence of frames from right to left, to compare any pair of individual plots, and to refer to the corresponding data inside the boxes. In other words, the reader is in control, and may learn at his own chosen rate. The animated film sequence, however, dictates both the manner and rate at which the viewer is presented with information. Success is totally dependent on the skill of the production team in devising and presenting the animation.

      If, in the histogram sequence, the action simply consisted of starting with the first plot and animating directly to the last, the eye would have little chance to examine the changing number in each right-hand box because attention would be drawn to the movement of the histogram. (Much depends on the relative rates of change. The converse could hold where a rapidly changing number draws attention away from the histogram). The solution adopted in this case was to identify the separate objectives:

1. to show the continuous nature of the variation,

2. to relate specific shapes to specific values of the parameter.

The ensuing design was first to depict various distributions corresponding to different values by stopping at key points and allowing the viewer time to scan the static picture. The animation was then repeated with an uninterrupted sequence. The intervening television studio pictures also displayed stills from the animation to keep the image alive, taking full advantage of the preceding visual exploration.

In designing animation, it is important to use static frames to allow the viewer to digest the information. It is wrong to assume that because information is displayed, the viewer will automatically absorb it.

Even with a carefully planned sequence, the viewer's eye may be drawn away from the places where we want attention focussed. In one calculus animation we wanted to show the way in which a 'derived function' was generated. The method was to draw a small tangent to a curve (if you like, the parent curve) and then cause it to progress along the curve like a toboggan which could follow both the uphill and downhill sections. The magnitude of the slope, or gradient, of the tangent was plotted as a second curve below the original. The idea was to get the tangent to travel smoothly from left to right and plot out this second curve. At the same time we wanted to point out that during the development, the x-values were the same for both curves.

The first design was rejected because it would not show conclusively that the two points corresponded to the same x-value.

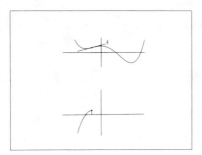

This was revised to incorporate a vertical dashed line (representing a common x-value) connecting the two points. This would serve to link the points for the eye and reinforce the spoken commentary.

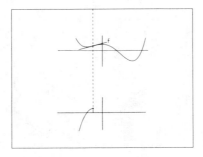

It was at this stage that the commission was finalised. We discovered that the eye is drawn up and down this vertical from top to bottom of the screen and so takes attention away from the critical points on the curves. In addition, the presence of the 'infinite' vertical line running off the screen in both directions, encouraged vertical eye movements which conflicted with the horizontal progression across the frame, making it difficult to concentrate on the animation. Terminating the dashed line at the two critical points allowed the eye to flick between them. In this way we concentrate on the crucial points on each curve and allow the horizontal movement to dominate:

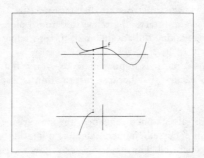

Using a dashed line created further potential for visual conflict. When used in conjunction with horizontal movement it is important to determine which end of the line will be fixed (i.e. the point from which the dashed pattern will commence). Because the length of the dashed line changes as it traverses the screen, dashes will appear and disappear. Hence a horizontal traverse will create a sense of vertical movement. In the preceding example there are three ways of creating the dashed line.

(i) Fixed point on the upper curve

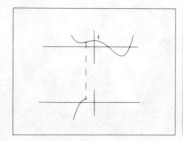 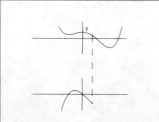 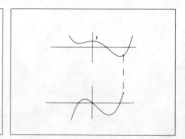

(ii) Fixed point on the lower curve

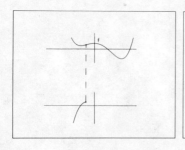 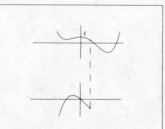 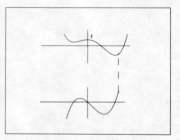

(iii) Dashed line fixed relative to frame

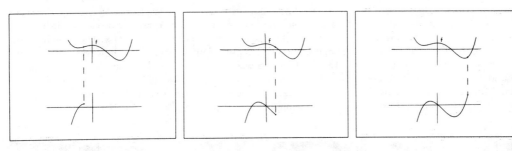

From the above stills (with exaggerated spacings of the dashed line) there is little apparent difference between them; in the animated sequence an amazingly pronounced effect appears. In (i) the line seems to hang down from the upper curve (A) to the the lower curve (B) and to 'grow' downwards as the distance between A and B increases. This reinforces the dominant role of A in the construction of B. From an intuitive mathematical point of view this is the correct image. In (ii) the pattern starts from the lower curve and appears to be resting on top of it. As the separation of A and B increases the line appears to 'grow' upwards and so conflicts with the image we are trying to convey. In the final case, (iii) the line will appear to grow at both ends at once, each dashed segment remaining at the same vertical displacement relative to the whole frame. Hence, in this case, it will not visually relate to its end points. More specifically it will appear that the dashed line is being viewed through a 'window' cut out to the shape formed between the two curves.

It is hidden pitfalls such as these which can be avoided through experience. Even with the simple case of joining two points by a dashed line one must consider carefully the effect that will be created.

Broken line patterns have many other applications, and one which has often been of value concerns the transformation of curves and shapes. When a curve is transformed we frequently leave a dashed image (occasionally a faint one) in its initial position. The viewers can, if we provide a static frame, compare the original position with the new one and recapitulate for themselves. We remove this when the sequence has progressed beyond the point where it is considered useful for the student to be reminded of the earlier history. This is illustrated on the storyboard shown earlier.

In each animation many minor details of this kind require careful consideration. They may have little significance for the total action, yet these apparently minor issues, if neglected, can result in such visual irritation that the image to be conveyed is completely destroyed. With experience, such pitfalls can be anticipated and correctly treated; many are concerned with the nature of computer calculations and operations. These are not in the province of the computer animator. These lessons are learned through experience and we hope that the length of our collaboration is reflected in our current work.

THE RIGHT TOOL FOR THE RIGHT JOB

At BBB-OUPC the aim is not to try to make computer graphics do everything, but to weld it into a presentation which will involve studio graphics, models, location film and conventional animation. Each of these resources has its own particular strengths: computer animation is undoubtedly the best for displaying 'mathematical' movement. We combine the computer generated film with studio presentation by using Colour Separation Overlay (CSO) and by synthesising colours from the black and white signal from the microfilm images.

For example, in the television programme on **Taylor Approximations**, we invented a 'function' machine which would depict any combination of the graphs of powers of x. The 'machine' was a working model with moving sliders and controls. Computer generated graphics, however, provided the answers for the set demonstrations. The final picture was a composite studio scene with the animation placed on the 'machine's' screen by colour separation overlay. (Incidentally, care had to be taken to match perspective, since, in the camera picture, the machine's screen was not square on, although the images to be inlayed on it were computed as though for a flat screen).

In the studio   What the viewer sees

Using this technique we were able to harness the power of computer animation to bring the mathematics to life and so to stimulate our students' interest and imagination.

Because, at the Open University, we do not have a lot of time or money, the producers have to use computer animation economically and so need to be sympathetic to its capabilities. We have learned to embed it in the programme and not ask for the moon. For example, we minimise annotations, as large numbers of TV-readable characters can be expensive in terms of computer and microfilm time. The same holds true for shading: we only use it when really needed. (It should be said that these considerations are to a large extent dictated by the available graphics system and would not necessarily apply elsewhere). Thus we use computer animation sparingly, returning to the studio for recapitulation and to keep the 'story' alive while giving the students a breather, or while progressing to the next stage in the story.

We keep computer animation sequences short for good production reasons. Long sequences which carry more than one concept may well lose our students. Also, computer animations can have a hypnotic quality and it is easy for the viewer to get swamped in detail. So from time to time in a programme, whatever device is being used to convey the message, we build in what we call signposts, recapitulations, or related demonstrations to give a different perspective but which repeat the same points. In short, we let out slower students catch up yet provide the quicker ones with an extra angle. Because of the density of information in computer animation, even the most hardy and devoted viewers can find they get punch drunk from time to time. We tend to use computer animation in short bursts and it is rare for us to use a computer generated sequence of much longer than three minutes. In fact, the short bursts can heighten the experience and we have made whole programmes built around them in this manner.

The computer animation is not, however, often used to tell the complete story. As a scarce resource, it must be used sparingly. Accordingly, computer animation is used for its strengths — to fascinate and to provide a visual solution to a problem posed previously in the programme, or where the mathematics is of such complexity that it is not feasible to draw an accurate picture by traditional methods. One way to sustain interest and tell a good story in a 25 minute programme is to weave several different ingredients together. These include presenters, studio graphics, studio models, conventional animation and computer animation. Each has its particular strength. Presenters develop the detailed storyline as well as providing signposts for continuity through the programme. The strength of computer animation is to reveal how the mathematics behaves.

THE FUTURE – WHERE DO WE GO FROM HERE?

At the BBC Open University Production Centre there is a computer-controlled video rostrum camera which allows graphics designers to embark on multiple-pass video recordings with facilities for roll back and re-mixing. Backgrounds can be recorded separately, colour separation overlay and inlay enable animated sections to be inserted and live action sequences incorporated. In the long term, with the prospect of coupling it to automatic character generators and frame stores, the video rostrum facility will be powerful.

The video rostrum is best used where the screen is composed from several different sources, each one being well suited for its particular use. At present we cannot feed computer animation into this system because of the unsteadiness of the 16mm frame. We have found that mixing the perfectly locked video signals with 16mm film just draws attention to this problem and is very distracting. Although technically possible, it is clearly not economic to use the present vector generated animation system at ULCC to provide shading and captions. Direct-to-video animation is not within our budgets; most of our applications are 'one-off' and cannot make much use of the 'menu' approach with the current generation of raster scan devices.

In the long term, perhaps, computing speeds and plotting speeds will have improved so much that we can go direct to video. But for the mid-term, the best hope is an interface direct to a frame store and to build up our animations frame by frame. We might perhaps be able to adapt to direct frame by frame recording on to broadcast quality helical scan equipment. With direct to video animation we shall be able to use the appropriate technology for the appropriate task. We will have the choice of vector or raster type displays, we will use the video rostrum for solid model and real life sequences, backgrounds and graphics. The character generators could be linked in as well.

It all sounds too good to be true, but we also have to be aware of being hypnotised by an increasingly complex array of facilities. When out national TV networks changed to colour, wise old men were heard to observe that many had not learned to use black and white properly. We also wonder whether the same will be true of computer graphics in education?

Vector displays have been around for well over 15 years and yet the educational world has not really taken full advantage of them. Perhaps it is because until the advent of the Open University mathematics and science courses with television as a built-in component the demand simply had not been there to any significant degree. In the Open University context, we were forced to use broadcasting, not to replace the lecturer, but to provide students with experiences that they had never seen before.

So whatever the developments in technology we must continue to press for clearer ways of presenting material. We must be economic in harnessing the power of these new dimensions. For example, movement is an essential ingredient, but we must avoid excesses — any movement must be worthwhile to the viewer, it must carry the message and it often needs a good deal of analysis to determine what the message really is.

The main problems in the future will not be the shortage of new technologies; they will be in the shortage of people capable of using them to the best effect.

In mathematics education many believe there are drawbacks in attempting to develop clearer ways of illustrating difficult concepts. It is easy to make the assumption that 'seeing' leads to 'believing' which in turn leads to understanding. If we make things too easy for our students there is a danger that they may be entertained but will not learn properly. In mathematics, and we suspect in many other areas too, there is no such thing as instant understanding. Often, true understanding can only come from the hours spent in the long, hard stuggle to master a topic. Many famous mathematicians have said that studying the hard way is the only way — and it is good for you. That is probably why there are some who fail to see much value in computer animation for education. All of these points are valid. The answer is not to pretend that the animations alone do the teaching. It is our experience that if the animations are sufficiently memorable they can be coupled to that other type of experience — learning the hard way. If the television images are strong enough, and if they are linked with the student's own mental images created when working through examples, the computer animation will have provided a valuable hook on which the student can hang abstract ideas.

We agree that whatever educational aids teachers use, students cannot avoid having to learn for themselves. We do believe, however, that the sort of animations that we have developed, coupled with good television presentation, can at least give them enormous help with the task.

REFERENCES TO BBC OPEN UNIVERSITY PROGRAMMES

Programmes in the M101 course which are referred to in this chapter are as follows:

Behaviour of Functions	M101/12F
Taylor Polynomials	M101/14F
Modelling Surveys	M101/23F
Complex Numbers	M101/26F
Mathematics : A Social Perspective/Case Study	
Catastrophe Theory	M101/32F

Details of costs and further information on the series may be obtained from:-

Open University Educational Enterprises Ltd
12 Cofferidge Close
Stony Stratford
Milton Keynes
MK11 1BY
UK

COMPUTER ANIMATION AS AN AID
TO COMPREHENDING THE UNIVERSE

Ken Knowlton

Bell Laboratories

Computer animation offers the possibility of providing an intellectual framework for understanding the relative magnitudes of time and of space. For every process, whether large or small, fast or slow, there will be an appropriate scale at which to view it, so that its salient features are clear. The chief task in understanding something is often to inter-relate these scales, and computer imaging may provide a novel way of facilitating this understanding.

Popularisers of science perform the noble service of acquainting us with things that are much larger and smaller than we can personally experience, and events which occur much more quickly or much more slowly than we can easily comprehend. But they often do a disservice, by implying "don't try to comprehend these time periods and sizes — they're beyond you." We are left with something like the '1, 2, 3, many' system of counting. Things smaller than a millionth of an inch are 'submicroscopic' and things farther away than the moon lie at 'astronomical' distances. Events shorter than a hundredth of a second happen at 'lightning' speed, whereas anything older than 5,000 years began eons ago — and don't bother to ask just exactly how long one eon is.

What I plan to sketch out here is a systematic way of giving more structure to the small and the large, the slow and the fast — a set of landmarks — so that we can relate more easily small things to each other, large things to each other, and make similar comparisons amongst the fast and the slow. In this system computer-drawn images can be very useful.

Scales of Space and Time

A grain of sand can be seen by the naked eye, but not a micro-organism; smaller than these cells are large molecules, then small molecules, then atoms; near the low end of the scale, at about 10^{-15} metre in size, we find the proton. Large objects we might consider are mountains, continents and oceans, the earth and the rest of the solar system star clusters and galaxies are some of the largest known objects and the entire observable universe must represent a limit. These sizes, along with those of a few other objects of interest, are plotted on a logarithmic scale in Fig. 1. The ratio of the largest to the smallest size indicated there is about 10^{40}.

Times for events of interest also range over nearly 40 orders of magnitude: the universe is

131

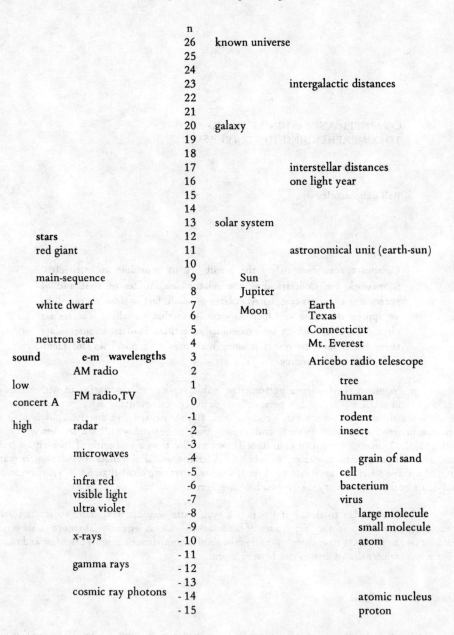

Fig. 1 Some sizes and distances of interest, plotted on a logarithmic scale.
Dimensions are 10^n metres for indicated values of n.

about 6×10^{17} seconds old, whereas half-lives of some isotopes are less than 10^{-18} seconds. These, and events of intermediate duration, are listed in Fig. 2. (We could extend this scale further: the suspected half-life of the proton is now estimated to be $\sim 10^{40}$ seconds, 10^{22} **times** the present age of the universe; light traverses a proton 3 times in 10^{-24} seconds).

Periods		n	Epochs	
		18	age of the universe	
		17	age of the earth	^{238}U lifetime
galactic revolution		16	since first dinosaurs	
		15	mammals	
		14	human species	
		13		
precession of Earth's axis		12	agriculture	
		11	recorded history	^{14}C lifetime
Pluto around Sun		10	human lifetime	
sunspot cycle		9	adolescence	
Earth around Sun		8		
Moon around Earth		7	school semester	
		6	long weekend	
Earth rotation		5	night's sleep	
satellite around Earth		4	lecture	
		3	tuning a guitar	
long traffic light		2		
slow breathing		1	orgasm	
heartbeat		0	voluntary reaction time	
TV frame		-1	eye blink	
		-2		
mosquito wingbeat	Concert A	-3		
TV line		-4		
	e - m	-5		
	AM radio	-6		μ lifetime
		-7	computer instruction	
	FM radio,TV	-8		
		-9		
	radar	-10		
		-11		
	microwaves	-12		
atom vibration		-13		
	infra red	-14		
	visible light	-15		
	ultra violet	-16		π^0 lifetime
		-17		
	x-rays	-18		
		-19		Σ^0 lifetime
	gamma rays	-20		
		-21		
	cosmic ray photons	-22		

Fig. 2.   Time durations of some periodic and non-periodic phenomena plotted on a logarithmic scale. Times are 10^n seconds for indicated values of n.

Combining space and time in a single notion, speed, we find again many things off the scale of direct experience. At the high end is the speed of light, and toward the low end we might consider the growth of a stalagmite in a limestone cave. These and other speeds of interest, are listed in Fig. 3.

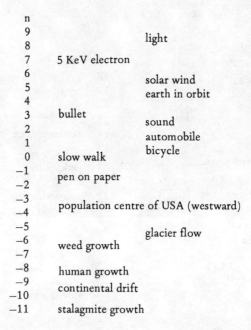

n		
9		light
8		
7	5 KeV electron	
6		
5		solar wind
4		earth in orbit
3	bullet	
2		sound
1		automobile
0	slow walk	bicycle
−1	pen on paper	
−2		
−3		
−4	population centre of USA (westward)	
−5		glacier flow
−6	weed growth	
−7		
−8	human growth	
−9	continental drift	
−10		
−11	stalagmite growth	

Fig. 3. Some speeds of interest, plotted on a logarithmic scale and expressed as 10^n metres/second for indicated n.

Cinematography

A few sciences, notably anatomy and taxonomy, concern themselves mainly with describing and classifying static objects. But most of the sciences consist of coming to terms with happenings; we are therefore compelled to use the moving media — movies and television — to depict them.

The most obvious way of capturing phenomena and showing them to others is to take movies of the actual events. And for things somewhat slow or fast, or large or small, we use special equipment. For short-lived events, for example, we use high speed cameras that take tens of thousands of pictures a second. But for speeds much faster than that we need extraordinary cameras; furthermore, we are limited to objects which can withstand extremely bright illumination, or events which are themselves brilliantly self-luminous. For things that happen very slowly we use time-lapse photography to speed them up by a factor of ten, a hundred, or a thousand, beyond which we begin to lose patience. Things that are vey small we photograph through microscopes, reaching a practical limit for living things at about 1,000x. Something large we back away from to get it entirely into view. But only some scenes can we conveniently back away from to photograph — for example, we are not yet able to take a picture of the solar system as a whole (and I for one cannot conceive of a way to photograph our own galaxy from the outside). The best that these methods of photography give us, then, is a way of expanding or compressing time and space to about a thousandfold from what we directly experience.

There is another serious limit to photography: it does not produce certain desirable abstractions. For example, in illustrating the evolution of the human skull, even with infinite patience and incredible foresight, time-lapse photography could not do the trick. In this instance, we want to see the change over a long period of time of an abstraction — the 'normal' skull, not the development of a particular skull over a period of time.

Computer Animation

The obvious way to extend our visual experience — into the more distant realms of time and space and into the abstract as well — is to use animation. Sequences of drawings, made to appear something like photos, but 'photographed' by an imaginary camera, sometimes have extraordinary abilities and properties. In dealing with scientific subject matter, it seems quite natural to use computer-drawn rather than hand-drawn pictures; since these objects are describable logically and mathematically, as soon as we have precisely described (programmed) a thing or an operation, we are in a position to make several film clips, using a variety of settings of the defining variables, including, of course, the dimensional scale factors and the rate at which time passes.

Computer animation also lends itself well to the regulation of a discipline — such as that suggested below — designed to smooth the transition between scales of observation and among a variety of authorships. And data links between computers facilitate collaborations and exchanges of software among geographically separated animators.

A Proposed Framework

One book and two films made by standard animation already stand out as impressive attempts to deal with the vast and the tiny; **Cosmic View: The Universe in 40 Jumps** by Kees Boeke, **Cosmic Zoom** by Robert Verrall and Joseph Koenig, and **Powers of Ten** by Charles and Ray Eames. What I propose here is an elaboration on these which Frank Sinden and I developed during the earlier days of computer animation. It uses a two-dimensional array of 'magical windows', some of which are illustrated in Fig. 4, through which we view the world (and more). At any moment our field of view on the movie screen contains what we can see through just one window. Let us experiment with the windows by taking an imaginary trip as follows:

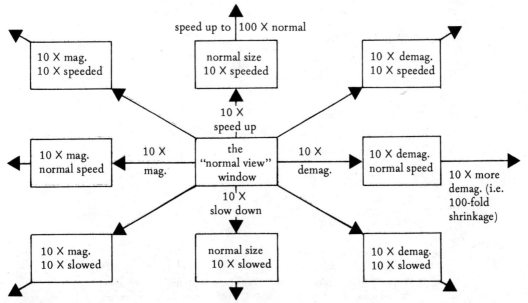

Fig. 4. Part of the array of windows for viewing events at indicated sizes and speeds.

We are in a limestone cave and we begin by looking through that special 'normal' window near the centre of our array – seeing a few stalactites and stalagmites and an occasional fellow speleologist walking across in front of us, appearing life-size and walking at normal speed. To get a wider view, we decide to look through the next window on the right – the 10 X demagnification window – and we do this by shifting the entire framework to the left. Our view is temporarily interrupted by the thick window frame but when it is re-established, everything is ten times smaller, including the people, who now appear 18 centimetres high. We see behind them the entire wall of the cave. Reversing the process, we come back to the original view, and then go one window further to the left where everything is enlarged by ten –whereupon we notice water dripping onto the rounded top of the stalagmite. For an even closer look, we view the scene at one hundred times magnification, one column still further to the left, and see huge drops of water smashing down. Remembering strobe pictures of water falling on wet surfaces, we slow down time by looking through the first and then the second window below, (moving the framework up!) achieving a time-dilation of one hundred times and see the crown-shaped splash. Finally, we want to see the stalagmite grow by crystallization of carbonate of lime from the water. As a first stab at this, we quickly shift the framework down nine steps so that we are now looking through the seventh row above normal speed – where in one second we see what normally takes four months – but nothing noticeable happens. Finally, when the window three rows higher is put in our line of view, we see (still at one hundred times enlargement) the stalagmite growing upward from the centre of the screen and out of our field of view in four seconds.

Now for each thing and phenomenon of the world and universe, there will be some appropriate viewing scale and rate, i.e. some particularly advantageous window through which to watch. A number of these are identified in Fig. 5. Some events are best followed through a series of viewpoints.

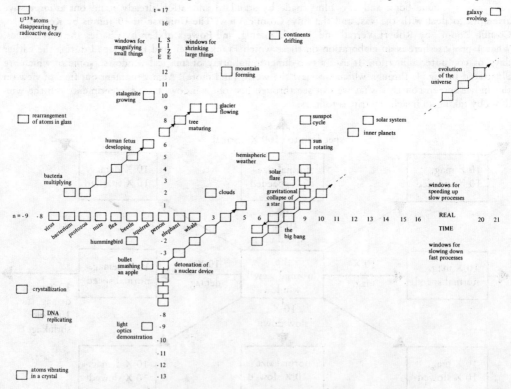

Fig. 5. Proposed viewpoints (windows) for observing a number of objects and phenomena. Field of view is 2×10^n metres wide for indicated n; time is speeded up by a factor of 10^t for indicated t.

General Observations

The use of our system deserves some general remarks. One is that a fixed speed can be observed through a number of windows diagonally adjacent — thus in their initial moments, the explosions of ‚a bomb or of the universe occupy small spaces (if the universe is finite); at later stages, if we want to see the expansion in its entirety, we must both enlarge our field of view and speed up the process.

Another result, not surprising, is that the commonly used windows as a group have a diagonal distribution. In particular, we will presumably never use the lower right region because, since nothing moves faster than the speed of light, we will never see motion there. (When we are animating waves fronts of light or objects moving at speeds approaching that of light, we will probably ignore relativity, and view by 'superlight' that travels instantaneously, and as if simultaneity had meaning).

Figure 5 deserves some scrutiny. It is the beginning of a conceptual map for finding our way around, so that we can begin to see new things from old and familiar vantage points. We soon learn that atoms are almost always observed nine or ten columns to the left, whereas the entire earth almost fills the screen seven columns to the right. Eventually our intellectual understanding of rates and magnitudes may become an experimental one as the action of our framework of windows itself becomes a believable fantasy. We have, moreover, a better way of telling certain stories that test our animation abilities: for example, the life story of a star, which exhibits a vast range of dimensions, with long periods of relative stability punctuated by cataclysmic events. (In addition to showing the macroscopic star, we might also show the corresponding energy conversion phenomena at molecular, atomic and nuclear scales). Where we are looking from, conceptually, is as important to the story as what we are seeing.

Work to be done

Some beautiful computer animation has already been done at various scales; for example, atoms forming crystals or galaxies of stars evolving. The atoms are usually shown as spheres and the stars as point masses and in both cases a rather simple force law — applied pair-wise — determines the motions. But the realm of things we must deal with is much vaster and more intricate; in order to do an adequate job and lend smoothness and credibility to our imaginary viewpoints, we Computer Animators must push in at least three directions: we need to bridge the gaps between our various data representations, we need to do better at depicting natural processes, including life, and we need to be able to make smoother transitions to and from live-action cinematography.

There are, of course, good reasons for each kind of representation that we commonly employ — usually a need for efficiency of description or of computation. It is nonsensical to make a building out of spheres or an atom out of blocks. But we do need transitions. For example, progressive magnification of a salt crystal, whose data structure and representation is originally polyhedral, ultimately yields atoms whose forms are likely to be spheres or thermal ellipsoids. Backing away (upwards) from a geometric city or airport, we may eventually want to be seeing images of clouds and weather patterns — these are not properly describable by hard-edge geometry.

We are probably more interested in processes of life than anything else — yet these are terribly difficult to reduce to logic and geometry. A human head may at times be represented by a sphere, a forearm by a cylinder, and a red cell by an ellipsoid, depending upon the purpose to be served. But if we have started with live action photography and switch to animation then we want a smooth enough transition to understand the mapping and continue the suspension of disbelief. Rightly or wrongly, our viewers will link authenticity of representation with authenticity of message.

In short, we really want to see things as if we were looking at the same phenomenon but with higher magnification, slowed pace, or whatever. If appearances change drastically at some moment — for example from smooth cubic patches to polyhedra, or vice versa — the jolt will cause us to lose the continuity in the plot.

There is another kind of research that needs to be done. The best ways of portraying the extent of the window-hopping needs to be established. The possible methods of visual presentation may include the development of ancillary aids. Audible tones might be used as a mnemonic. For example, 14 notes in an ascending chromatic scale, with every fourth note accented, in synchronism with 14 jumps to the right on the frame, should be clearly remembered as 14 (not 13 or 15) orders of demagnification. Instead, or in addition, the window frames themselves, marked in some way with row and column designations, might always show slightly.

Similarly, a visual notation for dealing with mixed scales has to be worked out. Imagine, for example, dealing with the earth-sun-moon system. At a scale where we get them all into the same picture (the plus 11 column) the moon is scarcely visible, since its radius is only 10^{-5} of the radius of the earth's orbit. We clearly need to display different things at their own appropriate scales, perhaps in the manner suggested by Fig. 6, where each internal frame in the picture signifies a 10 times magnifying glass, a double frame (or perhaps a frame labelled $-2-$) means one hundred times, etc. With some experience I expect people to develop an intuitive skill at understanding such pictures, even to the point of being able to add another frame in Fig. 6 labelled $-6-$, meaning a further 10^6 magnification to show the magnitude of the tide on the open ocean (less than one metre in actual height). I believe — but don't yet have convincing evidence — that this sort of animation illustrating the seasons of the year, eclipses, tides, etc., will be felt to be more authentic and thus understandable and believable, than the grotesque, though unmentioned, distortions we typically find in explanatory diagrams.

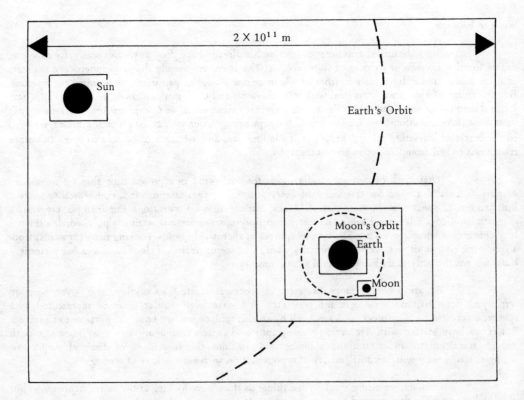

Fig. 6. Example of mixed scales. Each internal frame indicates a 10 X enlargement.

Keeping Perspective

The universe is magnificent. And there is nothing in our treatment that should change the sense of awe or wonder which we feel when trying to experience these times and spaces. With time speeded up by a factor of 10^{10}, a human lifetime goes by in a quarter of a second; at this scale the human race has been around for 2 hours and the universe for two years. With space shrunk by 10^{10}, the earth is a pinhead, the sun is a grapefruit 15 metres away, and the next nearest star is 4,000 kilometres distant. Each step from window to window is a big step, and our intellectual excursions take us through many steps.

What we are trying to do, using this method of representation, is to provide an intellectual framework for remembering how big and small the very large and microscopic things are. Likewise, we hope to be able to remember long and short expanses of time and extremes of speed. Finally, we want to relate phenomena to each other — facilitating, for example, our understanding of which wavelengths of illumination we need for seeing which sizes of objects or detail.

We should have added to the list of our experiences the pleasure of playing with a new toy; it is as if our observation windows are a set of very special places to sit, or 'scopes to look through'. With increasing experience, some of these 'scopes will become familiar, or remain odd, depending upon how often, or for what purpose, we use them.

Science is the study of **processes**. In the past, most pictures and diagrams in textbooks and journals have been single frames from movies that were never made. Not only are we now in a position to start making these films, I think we can also put them into a more coherent conceptual framework.

References

Boeke, K (1957) **Cosmic View : The Universe in 40 Jumps**, John Day, New York.

The films referred to in this chapter are listed in Appendix A.

APPENDIX A   **FILMS**

Readers in search of computer-animated films are recommended to obtain the invaluable listing known as **An International Guide to Computer-Animated Films.** Compiled by Rick Speer, Bill and Ruth Kovacs, it was first published in 1979. Copies are available price $5.00 plus 60c. for US postage. (European readers should add more for postage) from:

> Animation Research
> P.O. Box 2651
> Seattle
> Washington 98111
> USA

We list below some items which may not appear in the Guide or which are specifically referred to in the chapters of this book.

1.   **Collision of Two Galaxies**
           Models of collision of two self-consistent galaxies.
           2 mins   16mm
           Rick Miller, University of Chicago

2.   **Cosmic Zoom**
           Probes infinite magnitude of space and its reverse, the ultimate minuteness of matter.
           8 mins   1968   16mm
           National Film Board of Canada

3.   **The Structure and Function of Haemoglobin**
           A computer-generated, 3-D (red-green anaglyph) movie with a ball-and-stick representation of the haemoglobin molecule. Includes zooms and rotations.
           25 mins   1980   16mm
           David R. Clark, University of London Audio-Visual Centre

4.   **Painting by Numbers**
           A videotaped discussion between Dr Jim Blinn and Dr Edwin Catmull, two pioneer computer animators, with some examples of their work.
           45 mins   1979   videocassette
           David R. Clark, University of London Audio-Visual Centre

5.   **Computer Simulation of Crystal Growth** and
           Nucleation on a Crystal Surface
           Two films which explore various crystal growth phenomena.
           12 mins and 8½ mins   silent   16mm
           George Gilmer, Bell Laboratories

6.   **Powers of Ten**
           Illustrates relationships between the number 10 and the size of the physical universe. Moves in real time over its course of 40 powers of ten, from the cosmic distances of the universe to the heart of an atom.
           9 mins   16mm
           Charles and Ray Eames

7.   **TRNA and DNA Models**
            Three-dimensional, coloured, shaded sequences of complex molecules based on Ken
            Knowlton's 'ATOMS' program.
            3 mins   1978   silent   16mm
            Nelson Max, Lawrence Livermore Laboratory

8.   **Voyager Flight Simulation**
            Simulation flight of the Voyager spacecraft past Jupiter. Views from the spacecraft and
            from a point outside the solar system.
            15 mins   1978   16mm
            Charles Kohlhase and Jim Blinn, Jet Propulsion Laboratory

Sources of material

1.   Rick Miller
            Dept of Astronomy
            University of Chicago
            5640 Ellis Avenue
            Chicago
            Illinois 60637
            USA

2.   NFBC
            16th Floor
            1251 Avenue of the Americas
            New York
            New York 10020
            USA

       or   Canada House Film Library
            Canada House
            Tragalgar Square
            London SW1
            UK

3 and 4   The Administrative Secretary
            University of London Audio-Visual Centre
            11 Bedford Square
            London WC1B 3RA
            UK

5   George Gilmer
            Bell Laboratories
            600 Mountain Avenue
            Murray Hill
            New Jersey 07974
            USA

6.   Pyramid Films
            Box 1048
            Santa Monica
            California 90406
            USA

7.   Nelson Max
          Lawrence Livermore Laboratory
          L-73
          Livermore
          California 94550
          USA

8.   Charles Kohlhase
          Jet Propulsion Laboratory
          264-443
          4800 Oak Grove Drive
          Pasadena
          California 91103
          USA

APPENDIX B   FURTHER READING

In a fast-changing field bibliographies are soon out-of-date. The suggestions below will give the reader some basic pointers to further reading but are by no means exhaustive.

1. ACM/SIGGRAPH quarterly reports on Computer Graphics 1974-80. Available from:

>   ACM Inc.
>   P.O. Box 12105
>   Church St Station
>   New York, NY 10249
>   USA

2. J. F. Blinn, **Computer Display of Curved Surfaces**, Ph.D. dissertation, University of Utah (1978).

3. K.S. Booth, (1979) ed. **Computer Graphics Tutorial**, IEEE Computer Society, New York.

4. J.P. Frisby, (1979) **Seeing : Illusion, Brain and Mind**, Oxford University Press.

5. W.K. Giloi, (1979) **Interactive Computer Graphics**, Prentice-Hall, Englewood Cliffs.

6. R.C. Gonzalez and P. Wintz, (1977) **Digital Image Processing**, Addison-Wesley, Mass.

7. R.W. Hunt, (Third edition 1975) **Reproduction of Colour in Photography, Printing and Television**, Halstead Press.

8. J. McKenzie, L. Elton and R. Lewis (eds) (1978) **Interactive Computer Graphics in Science Teaching**, Ellis Horwood, Chichester.

9. W.M. Newman and R. Sproull, (Second edition 1979) **Principles of Interactive Computer Graphics**, McGraw-Hill, New York.

10. Television Standards — PAL

>   a) Independent Broadcasting Authority Technical Review 2.
>   Second edition 1974. 70 Brompton Road, London SW3 1EY.

>   b) H.W. Sims (1976) **Principles of PAL Colour TV and Related Systems**, Newnes-Butterworth, London.

11. Television Standards — NTSC

>   a) CCIR Report 624-1 (Colour systems). From ITU Geneva, place des Nations, CH 1211 Geneva 20, Switzerland.

>   b) H.E. Ennes (1971) **Television Broadcasting**, Foulsham-Sams, Indianapolis and Slough (UK).

APPENDIX C

ADDRESSES OF SOME MANUFACTURERS OF EQUIPMENT
WITH THEIR SUBSIDIARIES

1. Displays

a) Vector

Evans & Sutherland
580 Arapeen Drive
Salt Lake City
Utah 84108
USA

Telephone: (801) 582-5847

Mecklenburger Str. 42
6200 Wiesbaden-Norderstadt
West Germany

011 49 6122 4659 (Ralph C.Harris)

Imlac Corporation
150 A Street
Needham
Ma 02194
USA

Telephone: (617) 449-4600

Imlac House
17 Chesham Road
Amersham
Bucks. HP6 5HN
UK

024 03 22167

Tektronix
P.O.Box 500
Beaverton
Oregon 97005
USA

Telephone: (503) 644-0161
Telex: 36-691

P.O. Box 69
36/38 Coldharbour Lane
Harpenden
Herts. AL5 4UP
UK

05827 63141
25559

Vector General, Inc.
21300 Oxnard Street
Woodland Hills
California 91367
USA

Telephone: (213) 346-3410

b) **Raster**

Advanced Electronics Design, Inc.
P.O. Box 61779
Sunnyvale
California 94088
USA

Telephone: (408) 733-3555
Telex: 357498

Aydin Controls
414 Commerce Drive
Fort Washington
Pa 19034
USA

Telephone: (215) 542-7800

Aydin Controls/Vector
Andre House
Salisbury Square
Hatfield
AL9 5BH
UK

07072 72771

Datec
Furrer Marketing SA
4 Cours des Bastions
CH-1205 Geneva
Switzerland

Telephone: 022-205133
Telex: 27237

Evans & Sutherland
(see above)

General Electric Company
Video Display Group
Electronics Park - Bldg 6
Syracuse
NY 13221
USA

Telephone: (315) 456-2562

International General Electric Co.
111 Park Road
London
NW8 7JL
UK

01 402 4100

Genisco Computers
17805 Sky Park Circle Drive
Irvine
California 92714
USA

Telephone: (714) 556-4916
Telex: 910-595-2564

b) Raster continued

Gresham Lion Ltd
Gresham House
Twickenham Road
Feltham
Middlesex
TW13 6HA
UK

Telephone: 01-884 5511
Telex: 27417

Grinnell Systems Corporation
2986 Scott Boulevard
Santa Clara
California 95050
USA

Telephone: (408) 988-2100

Techex Ltd
Braidley House
St Paul's Lane
Bournemouth
BH8 8HN
UK

0202 293115

Interpretation Systems Inc.
6322 College Boulevard
Overland Park
Kansas 66211
USA

Telephone: (913) 642-8700
Telex: 42285

Lexidata Corporation
215 Middlesex Turnpike
Burlington
Ma 01803
USA

Telephone: (617) 273-2700
Telex: 710-332-1381

Optronics International, Inc.
7 Stuart Road
Chelmsford
Ma 01824
USA

Telex: 94-7443

b) Raster continued

Process Peripherals GL Ltd
The Broadway
Thatcham
Berkshire
RG13 4HP
UK

Telephone: 0635-62229
Telex: 847417

Ramtek
585 North Mary Avenue
Sunnyvale
California 94086
USA

Telephone: (408) 735-8400

SEIN
Societe d'Electronique et d'Instrumentation
  Numerique
171 rue Veron
94140 Alfortville
France

Telephone: 375 98 31
Telex: SEIN 210572 F

Sigma Electronic Systems Ltd
Church Street
Warnham
Horsham
Sussex RH12 3QW
UK

Telephone: 0403-50445
Telex: 87323

Three Rivers Computer Corp.
160 North Craig Street
Pittsburgh
Pa 15213
USA

Telephone: (412) 621-6250

2. Image processing systems

Comtal Corporation
P.O. Box 5087
Pasadena
California 91107
USA

Telephone: (213) 797-1175
Telex: 910-588-3256

M & S Europe B.V.
P.O. Box 7708
1117 ZL Schiphol-Oost
Amsterdam
The Netherlands

020-47 24 67
10152

DeAnza Systems Inc.
118 Charcot Avenue
San Jose
California 95131
USA

Telephone: (408) 263-7155

Floating Point Systems, Inc.
P.O. Box 23489
Portland
Oregon 97223
USA

Telephone: (503) 641-3151
Telex: 360470

Floating Point Systems, SA Ltd
Dudley House
High Street
Bracknell
Berkshire
UK

0344-56921
(851) 849218

$I^2 S$
Stanford Technology Corporation
650 North Mary Avenue
Sunnyvale
California 94086
USA

Telephone: (408) 737-0200
Telex: 348467

Hunting Survey Services
Elstree Way
Boreham Wood
Herts
UK

Interpretation Systems Inc.
(see above)

Micro Consultants Ltd
Interface House
Croydon Road
Caterham
Surrey CR3 6QD
UK

Telephone: Caterham 48921   Telex: 946643

3. Microfilm plotters

Calcomp
2411 West La Palma Avenue
Anaheim
California 92801
USA

Telephone: (714) 821-2011
Telex: 910-591-1154

Calcomp
Cory House
The Ring
Bracknell
Berkshire
UK

0344-50211
848949

Dicomed Corporation
9700 Newton Avenue South
Minneapolis
Mn 55431
USA

Telephone: (612) 887-7100

M & S Europe B.V.
(see above)

Information International Inc.
5933 Slauson Avenue
Culver City
California 90230
USA

Telephone: (213) 390-8611
Telex: 910-343-6482

4. Video processing

Michael Cox Electronics Ltd.
Hanworth Trading Estate
Hampton Road West
Feltham
Middlesex
UK

Telephone: 01-898 6091
Telex: 935147

Quantel Ltd
Interface House
Croydon Road
Caterham
Surrey CR3 6QD
UK

Telephone: Caterham 48921
Telex: 946643

APPENDIX D

SOME FACILITIES COMPANIES

Computer-Aided Design Centre
Madingley Road
Cambridge, CB3 0HB
UK

0223 63125
Gordon Freeman

Cambridge Interactive Systems Ltd
Quayside
Cambridge, CB5 8AB
UK

0223 62247
Dick Newell

Computer Image Corporation
2475 W. 2nd Avenue
Suite 4
Denver
Colorado 80223
USA

(303) 934 5801
Ed Tajchman

Digital Effects Inc.
321 W. 44 Street
New York, NY 10036
USA

(212) 581 7760
Judson Rosebush

Grove Park Animations Ltd.
104 Grove Park
London SE5 8LE
UK

01-274 5395
Alan Kitching

Image West Ltd
845 North Highland Avenue
Hollywood
California 90038
USA

(213) 466 4181
Sonny King

Information International Inc.
5933 Slauson Avenue
Culver City
California 90230
USA

(213) 390 8611
John Whitney Jnr.

Logica Ltd
64 Newman Street
London W1A 4SE
UK

01-647 9111
Tony Diment, William Newman

MAGI Inc.
3 Westchester Plaza
Elmsford
New York 10523
USA

(914) 592 8322

Moving Picture Co. Ltd.
25 Noel Street
London W1
UK

01-734 9151

New York Institute of Technology
P.O. Box 170
Wheatley Road
Old Westbury
New York 11568
USA

(516) 686 7644
Louis Schure

Rutherford Laboratory
Chilton
Didcot
Oxfordshire OX11 0QX
UK

02352 1900
Paul Nelson

Software Generation Ltd.
50 - 51 Russell Square
London WC1
UK

01-458 6644
Tony Pritchett

System Simulation Ltd.
50 - 51 Russell Square
London WC1
UK

01-637 1169
John Lansdowne

University of London Computer Centre
20 Guilford Street
London WC1N 1DZ
UK

01-405 8400
Bob Colvill